AF646716

MORAL VALUES IN CHILDREN

About the Authors

Sushma Batra has done her doctorate from the Department of Social Work, University of Delhi. She Joined the Department, her alma mater in 1982 as a lecturer. At present she is a professor in the same Department. She has published six books. She also has to her credit more than 25 articles published in leading National and International Journals. She has been an academician of repute who has contributed widely to the profession by being an excellent teacher as well as a researcher especially interested in working with the People with disabilities, Older Persons, children and Adolescents. She has been the Honorary Director at the Centre for Child and Adolescent Well-being (CCAW), earlier known as child guidance centre for many years. The present compendium is the outcome of her joint research with Ms. Charu Sethi and the interns placed for the field work practicum over a period of three years at the CCAW. Earlier also she has published a book *Turbulent Teens: Approaches to Adjustment* published by the Mittal Publications.

Charu Sethi is pursuing PhD from University of Delhi. She has acquired a Diploma in Early Childhood Care and Education, IGNOU, Certificate in Professional Practices in Inclusion: Aspects of Learning Difficulties for Children and Young People with Disabilities from Roehampton University (U.K.), Certificate in Counselling and Professional Practice, DU. She has eight years of experience of working as a Social Worker in Child Guidance Centre, where she has worked with children and adolescents in schools, communities and centre for their well-being. She has worked with children individually and in groups on different aspects of life skills, behaviour management, supportive mental health programmes and many more. Ms. Sethi has organized regular summer camps for children in vacations and various seminars for their parents.

Saryu Gruschow is an early childhood educator, who currently resides in Chicago, USA, and teaches pre-kindergarten at Chicago Public Schools. She graduated from Columbia University with Masters in Early Childhood Education. Before moving to the United States, she worked with schools and international non-profits in New Delhi, to advance educational practices relating to girl child education, social service learning, and reading skills. She also holds a Masters in Social Work from the Department of Social Work, University of Delhi; and a Bachelors in Sociology from Hindu College, University of Delhi.

MORAL VALUES IN CHILDREN

A Compendium for the Facilitators

By

Sushma Batra
Charu Sethi
Saryu Gruschow

CONCEPT PUBLISHING COMPANY PVT. LTD.
NEW DELHI-110059

© Authors

All rights reserved. No part of this work may be reproduced, stored, adapted, or transmitted in any form or by any means, electronic, mechanical, photocopying, micro-filming recording or otherwise, or translated in any language, without the prior written permission of the copyright owner and the publisher. The book is sold subject to the condition that it shall not, by way of trade or otherwise, be lent, resold, hired out, or otherwise circulated without the prior publisher's written consent in any form of binding or cover other than that in which it is published.

The views and opinions expressed in this book are author(s) own and the facts reported by him/her have been verified to the extent possible, and the publishers are not in any way liable for the same.

ISBN-13: 978-93-86682-71-0

First Published 2018

Published and Printed by

Concept
Since 1974

Concept Publishing Company Pvt. Ltd.
A/15-16, Commercial Block, Mohan Garden
New Delhi-110059 (India)
T : +91 11 25351460, +91 11 25351794
E : publishing@conceptpub.com; *W*: www.conceptpub.com

Cataloging in Publication Data--Courtesy: D.K. Agencies (P) Ltd. <docinfo@dkagencies.com>

Batra, Sushma, 1953- **author.**

Moral values in children : a compendium for the facilitators / by Sushma Batra, Charu Sethi, Saryu Gruschow.

pages cm

Includes bibliographical references.

ISBN 9789386682710

1. Moral education (Elementary)--India. 2. Values--Study and teaching--Activity programs--India. 3. Etiquette for children and teenagers--India. I. Sethi, Charu, author. II. Gruschow, Saryu, author. III. Title.

LCC LC315.I4B38 2018 DDC 370.1140954 23

PREFACE

Since time immemorial, we have emphasized on the values such as harmony, peace, kindness, humility... respect for human dignity and human rights as well as respect for the elders are core values that need to be practised. Moral education aid as road map to guide children along a route to live life based on moral principles which are important both for the individual as well as for the society.

This framework serves a blue print to help school personnel to improve their understanding and practices in providing holistic education for children in a systematic and focused way. The preparation of this framework has undergone a wide and intensive consultation and feedback from the experts, educational practitioners and school administration. Their valuable suggestions and insights helped in improving the content as well in identifying values and creating evidence based practice. The comments and feedback received reinforced the contents as well as approach adopted in the compendium. The book has been organised under two sections. The first section illustrates about the moral values; its need, significance and how educators can use this manual. The second section comprises the sessions and activities in relation to eleven core values—Respect, Acceptance, Peace, Honesty, Humility, Kindness, Forgiveness, Obedience, Patience, Responsibility and Sincerity.

ACKNOWLEDGEMENTS

All the authors experience a deep feeling of accomplishment after the long awaited academic pursuit is over and the outcome of constant hard work is ready to see the light of the day. The last assignment on the agenda to be handled with utmost devotion and affection is to write few lines expressing gratitude to those few who have been with the authors in many ways in their hard and dedicated journey throughout the process.

We experienced the similar emotions after our module on value education was successfully practiced for three long years with the children studying in two schools. The experiment was undertaken in the natural environment with the children of primary sections in three different schools—two being run by the government and the other one being a convent school in North Delhi. It all began by conducting focus group discussion with six to eight experts from different disciplines, like education, anthropology, phycology and selected students from the department of social work. After a thorough whole day brain storming session, 11 moral values were identified. Thereafter, began the task of identifying different activities under each value. These were carried over in the school and modified a number of times till the principal, teachers and the student trainee felt in unison that the activity could rightly have the positive impact on the students. The same activity was repeated in the following two years with the different student trainees from Social Work Department placed for fieldwork practicum at the Centre for Child and Adolescent Well-Being of the Department of Social Work, University of Delhi. Thus, the reliability and validity of the module has been appropriately tested over a period of three long years. The activities have been designed in the most innovative manner using different modes. The module is ready to be used by the social workers, counsellor, parents and teachers in an attempt to inculcate the right values in small children.

The first and the foremost individual to be complimented in this endeavour is Ms. Saryu Gruschow who was the first fieldwork trainee during the span of three years and the responsibility of conducting focused group discussion and then identifying various activities and actually carrying them in the school during the first year. She also shouldered the responsibility to document the first draft of the module by collecting suitable pictures and pasting them. The other students who actively contributed in identifying values and then suggesting activities have been Ms. Maninder, Mr. Nikhil Gopal Aggarwal and Mr. Digvijoy. We express our special thanks to all of them.

We are grateful to the principal Mrs. Garima Bharti of DU Social Service Centre, Maurice Nagar, the Principal of M.C.D. Primary School, Majnu Ka Tila and the Principal of St. Xavier School, Civil Lines for permitting our students to practice in their school over a span of three years. The module in the present form has become possible only because of their timely cooperation.

Our special appreciation to Mr. Rahul, another student (2015-17 batch) of the Department of Social Work who helped us in modifying some of the activities under different values and making them more culture specific.

We would like to express our heartfelt thanks to dear Dr. Reena Merin Cherian and Dr. Tushti Bhardwaj for going through the entire draft and suggesting significant, though minor modifications in the module.

Our special thanks to the little children of three schools—our subjects, who are the reason for creating the module in the present form. Finally, yet importantly our thank to the publisher Mr. Ashok Kumar Mittal has been our chief inspiration, who motivated us in finishing the assignment with full passion. He is responsible for ensuring the timely publication of the compendium. I have reasons to believe that the module is apt in the present time when the families are undergoing transformation. It will prove very useful with the children of all the primary classes. The process of inculcating right values can be attained by the educators in most interactive manner involving all the beneficiaries. The module can be very effectively used by all the Schools of Social Work in strengthening their fieldwork and can be used by all the trainees places in the school setting as part of their field work.

Dr. Sushma Batra

Ms. Charu Sethi

Ms. Saryu Gruschow

CONTENTS

SECTION A

1
WHY MORAL VALUES?

1.1 WHAT ARE MORAL VALUES?

" What are values?"

" Why are they so important in the life of all human beings?"

" What is the difference between positive and negative values?"

" How are they inculcated?"

" What is the age when they should be imparted to children?"

" Who should impart values to these growing buds?"

" And which is the best method to impart values to children?"

The above listed deliberations, questions and anxieties cloud young parents when their child apply for admissions in formal school and enter the school gates for the first time holding tightly their hands. "Will our child develop as a good human being and possess all positive values?" With these apprehensions parents admit their child in a school setting expecting that the school is one of the most significant agency of socialisation to foster the right values in children.

The apprehensions are absolutely valid and relevant since the age of embedding positive and appropriate values is appropriate from a very early age, this could be validated from the assertions by several development professionals. The family is, of course, the first agency followed closely by the second most important agency which happens to be the school.

Values portrayed by us are the mirror images of personality possessed by each one of us. They are the reflection of what kind of a human being we are. They serve as markers to tell us that our life is heading in the right direction. When our actions and words are aligned with our values, we feel content, confident and satisfied. Thus values are the cherished beliefs and standards for right and wrong. They provide direction and meaning to life. They are believed to be fundamentals to inspire constructive behaviour and the persons possessing right values are believed to have a positive attitude in life. They are the guiding principles that govern the various actions of each one of us in our day-to-day functioning and behaviour.

The values owned by us most conform to the norms held by the society at a particular time. They are mostly derived from society, government, religion or the family to which the individual belongs. Values are dynamic. They are usually influenced by the changing philosophical ideologies, cultural and religious perspectives, social, political and geographical conditions. In modern emerging society, there has been a revolutionary change in the domain of values due to the influence of modern culture and globalization. Values are sedimented forms of morality which are set rules laid down by the society and social agencies. We acquire values gradually based on our cognitive, social and emotional development. In this relation it is interesting to see the significance of imparting moral or value education in school years of children.

1.2 KOHLEBERG'S MODEL OF MORAL DEVELOPMENT AND VALUES

Level	Age range	Description
Obedience/Punishment	Infancy	No difference between doing the right things and avoiding punishment.
Self-Interest	Pre-school	Interest shifts to rewards, efforts are made to secure greatest benefits for oneself. This is the stage where moral development and value education could influence the cognition of the child.

Level	Age range	Description
Conformity	School age	Becoming the 'good girl/boy image, here children make efforts to secure appreciation of others. Like previous stage this is also an important stage for developing conformity.
Authority and Social order	School age	The purpose of morality is maintaining the social order
Social contract	Teens	Mutual benefit and reciprocity, individuals start applying the learnt value systems here
Universal Principles	Adulthood	Morality reaches a level where personal and mutual benefits transcend

It is evident that level I and III are important with regard to value and value education as children start developing the concepts of rights and wrong and at this development stage adequate scaffolding can help children internalise the value systems and empathise.

1.3 VALUE EDUCATION

Value education means inculcating sense of humanism, a deep concern for the well-being of self, others and society at large. This can be accomplished only when we instil desired values at a young age when the mind is receptive and more adaptable. This would mean building strong character that they would have stability and not hesitate in taking correct decision even in difficult times.

Thus, value education is a planned educational intervention aimed at the development of personality and character of individuals. Our action and thought of ours leaves strong impression on our minds which determine our behaviour at a given moment and our response to a given situation. The sum total of all our impressions is what determines our character. Our past determines present and our present thoughts and actions will shape the future. This is a key principle for building the personality of any individual.

For building the personality and inculcation of right values, the educationists must keep in mind that individuals need to be educated at a very young age. As already stated, the two most basic socialization agencies in the life of all children are 'Home' and 'School'. Families and parenting play an important role in shaping the lives of the children. They help them in building their character. After some time, it is the school where all children spend significant years of their lives. The teachers play a significant role after parents in transforming their lives and inculcating desires values.

Imparting value education at school is essential for character building and life skills curriculum, customised specifically to address, in age appropriate and culture appropriate ways, the needs of children. It addresses the importance of worldview, which shapes child's values and behaviour as well as those of the society at large. The goal is to encourage the development of character which results in behaviour that will be beneficial not only to the individual in his/her own life but also to the lives of his/her fellow human beings. The objectives are to transfer to students knowledge (what to do and why); skills (how to do it) and desire (to do it). Value education gives young people sensible reasons to abstain from degrading values, to make informed decisions regarding their future.

1.4 NEED, SIGNIFICANCE, RATIONALE AND METHODOLOGY

1.4.1 The Need for Value Education

Children of late are increasingly being exposed to images of violence, experiencing various social problems due to the changing family structure. In early days most of the physical and emotional needs of the children were met by the joint family. The grandparents, aunts and uncles were always a constant source of support. However with the breakdown of joint family and emergence of nuclear family, decreasing family size and both parents working, the children are left to be cared by maids or day care centres. This has made them more vulnerable to all the risks in their daily lives. This is further supplemented by the acts of domestic violence, alcoholism, delinquency and deviance that they witness in and around themselves in the family and community. The weakening family bonds has also resulted in the formation of pressure groups within which children are more vulnerable to the influences of friends and peers and are at the risk of making the wrong decisions in life. This has further been aggravated by the increased exposure to media and internet access at a very young age. It becomes a time of utter confusion when a child seeks answers to questions like "Who am I?", "Who are my friends?", "What do I want?", "What is good or bad for me?"etc. They experience a dominant physical and emotional change, and are in the process of understanding themselves.

At the crucial phase in life, children need to be guided in how to develop their personality and character, where lack of moral guidance can have a direct bearing on what children can become and what they can become in the later years of their life. The early years in the school is the best time to inculcate moral values and build their character towards their potential. It attempts to create caring and respectful environments where students feel safe and emerge as a more confident individuals. Thus value education is seen to be effective not only in decreasing violence and bullying but also in creating more caring, cooperative, respectful and responsible human beings.

1.4.2 Significance

The significance of value education programme lies in the accepted research finding that children of the given age (primary and secondary) are especially receptive to cooperative ways of interacting and a value-based atmosphere. They enjoy learning about the values and learn positive social communication skills easily. Children function at their best in a nurturing environment of respect, patience and clear rules rather than of blame, shame and anger. They enjoy expressing their thoughts and feelings and being acknowledged. Their vocabulary, ability to think constructively and critical thinking skills develop along with social skills, emotional growth and self-esteem.

1.4.3 Rationale

It is recognised that through moral education programme, the cognitive thinking skills, social and emotional skills that students would be exposed to and asked to explore and develop, will help them grow towards their potential, protect them from violence and help them engage in the community with respect, confidence and purpose. What children learn through the intensive programme in the school would later be woven into the fabric of the society and environment.

1.4.4 Methodology

The present module is an outcome of continuous intensive work undertaken by the team members of the Centre for Child and Adolescent Well-being (CCAW) a Centre being run as the demonstration project by the Department of Social Work, University of Delhi. The centre provides diagnostic, treatment and referral services to children, adolescents and their family members. It also caters to the neighbouring schools and community focusing on preventive and promotive well-being programmes for the better mental health of children. The Centre trains students of social work profession both from bachelors and masters course. These students are also engaged in neighbouring schools to conduct weekly sessions on moral and ethical values with children. The need was felt to come up with the standard activity module comprising different ethical life skills in relation to our Indian social culture.

The Director and Social Worker of the Centre took this initiative sincerely and convened a focused group discussion by inviting six to eight experts from different fields, like education, anthropology, school principals, teachers, counsellors and student representatives of both government and private schools. After a thorough whole day brain storming session, prime set moral values were identified.

Those identified values were put to practice in primary classes of three schools through the structured activities for three years. These value based activities were conducted with the students of third and fourth class for the whole year who in turn gave performances in the morning assembly once every week before all the children of the school. The activities were modified depending on the feedback received from the teachers. After whole year of practice a feedback session was conducted with the principals, selected group of teachers and the beneficiary students. The teachers as well as the principals were of the view that the value based activities had benefited the children. This was probably the result of display of activities fostering positive values. In the next two years, the experiment was replicated and found to again bear positive results thereby enhancing the reliability quotient in the research which was carried out in the most scientific manner.

The module in the present form is available to the teachers of all the schools to use it for inculcating right values in the children of primary classes.

1.5 GUIDELINES FOR EDUCATORS

Educators being a significant source of knowledge and facilitator in inculcating good values work endlessly to foster the desirable characteristics amongst students. The foremost duty and responsibility of all educators is to ensure that all students develop the desirable characteristics or moral values apart from getting traditional education in the school in their primary classes. The education will lead them to become better academicians whereas the inculcation of good moral values will transform them to be a good human being.

The most desirable values include—

- **Honesty**: Honesty and integrity are very important in life. In the classroom students must be taught not to cheat on tests, not to copy classmates' homework, and not to tell lies to the teacher and others. The educator can guide students to be honest by setting a good example in class. The instructor should always be honest in his dealings with the class.
- **Enthusiasm for Learning:** Every educator wants students to love school and be eager to learn. Nothing is worse than having an unhappy child who doesn't want to come to school and feels bored. Every day the child should look forword coming to the school with more enthusiasm and learning should become a play activity for him/her classroom. In generating enthusiasm for learning, an educator must be a good motivator. The educator can do this by creating a very interesting classroom environment, and by using textbooks and other audio-visual materials which are fun to hear, read, and study. The educator can also be dynamic in class in his or her relationship with students.

- **Ambition and Hard Work:** Thomas Edison once said that genius is 10 per cent inspiration and 90 per cent perspiration. Anyone who really wants to achieve a goal has to set his or her mind to it, and work at it. Ambition and hard work must begin in the schools and classrooms. Students must not be allowed to be lazy, and they should be required to complete all assignments on time. A good educator gets students ambitiously working hard by offering them rewards. These rewards would include comments such as "excellent" or "nicely done" on tests and assignments. They also would include recognition for being number one in the class or getting the highest grade on a test. An educator can do this by announcing the highest achieving student in class or by posting their names on the classroom bulletin board, for example, as being student of the month.
- **Curiosity and Asking Questions:** Curiosity is a desirable characteristic which is missing from many students. There are just too many pupils who accept everything they hear or read and don't question its veracity. Many students have never learned how to ask questions to find out more about a topic they are studying. An educator could facilitate a student-centred classroom and teach inductively.
- **Being Responsible:** Responsibility is one of the most important desirable characteristics for students. Being responsible and held accountable for one's actions is a necessary behaviour for all members of society. There is no better place than the classroom to learn being responsible. Students must be responsible and held accountable for bringing their books and school supplies to class, turning in assignments on time, making up missed assignments, and being punctual to class. As for all desirable characteristics, the educator sets a good example by being punctual to class and having all of his lessons prepared. There should be both rewards and punishments for ensuring the responsibility of students. The punishments could include staying after class or doing extra assignments.
- **Self-Esteem:** If a student is going to care about others and display good manners, he or she should have self-esteem. Students must learn to love themselves and take pride in their appearance and

clothing. They must feel good about themselves and have self-confidence. Here the educator can play a big part in developing a student's self-esteem. The educator can do this by showing concern and love for the student, and by giving the student attention and every opportunity to succeed.

- **Co-operation with others:** Working with others is a necessary part of classroom life. In fostering a good learning environment, it is worthwhile for students to join in discussion groups and work together on projects. A educator sets an example by showing them how to work together on a class project. Students could also observe a educator working closely with another educator in team teaching.
- **Being kind and helpful:** Students can exhibit this by doing classroom tasks such as erasing the board for the educator or helping him or her pass out books and papers. A kind and helpful student will also tutor weaker students in class. A educator sets an example by being kind and helpful to his students.
- **Being Public-Minded:** Public-mindedness is a desirable characteristic for everyone in society. There is no better place than school to develop this civic responsibility. Students should be expected not to litter, and to volunteer to carry benches and chairs to be set up for a school assembly. Educators can develop this desirable behaviour by setting a good example by not littering and picking up trash in public areas. A good educator could also show his students films about pollution and global warming and discuss these topics.

In preparing students for their roles in society, the development of desirable characteristics or moral values of students cannot be overlooked. If educators avoid this responsibility, in the future there will be more deviant behaviour problems in society.

1.6 HOW EDUCATORS CAN USE THIS MANUAL

Children are easily being exposed to images of violence, social problems and disrespect. This leads to gruesome implications in their daily lives, changing family ties, emotional bonds and their moral and social values. Through the value education module, students will be able to explore and develop their cognitive thinking, social and emotional skills.

The present module is meant to use by trained educators of Primary department of schools. Activities in the module are designed to be executed in the classroom setting. It targets children of age group 8 to 12 years.

In a classroom environment, educators foremost aim should be to establish an atmosphere of trust and respect with students/children. He/she must understand the background of children and mould the sessions to suit their learning capacities. Educator shall support children and should prevent any conflict between children (if occurs) and resolve it in agreement with all. Encouraging children for interaction and participation is important, educator can jumble the activities of one session in continuation.

Educator can also take session in an interactive manner to sustain the interest of the children. They can:

- Listen and observe carefully during the session.
- Focus on the learning of individual participants rather than finishing.
- Appreciate students in various ways—Big and Small.
- Assign classroom jobs.
- Hand over some control.
- Reward positive behaviour.
- Facilitate circle times.

1.7 IMPORTANT CONSIDERATIONS

- This module is meant for use by educators and to be used in classroom or group setting.
- The module targets children of age group of 8 to 12 years and with the group of 30 to 35 children.
- The author had selected particular values after discussions, research etc.
- The author had also selected particular poems, stories, resource material after discussions etc.—there could be many more otherwise.

- Other ideas and activities could be developed and used to supplement these.
- One could modify sessions by adding to/using alternative activities to suit the specific context.
- Most activities have been taken from various resource material and ideas available in published books and internet sites—we have compiled for easy programme and implementation—so that they are effective and easy to implement and accomplish through this easy-to-use manual.
- Every value session has a common thread of three basic objectives.
- Activities overlap for various values—many values in one activity (or at least more than one).
- You could find many stories and poems all over—use them at all times to supplement these exercises.
- It all depends on facilitation.
- One could jumble activities as per time availability but strongly recommended to hold and complete activities of one session in continuation.
- We tried to simplify but you could improvise.

SECTION B: THE MODULE

Name of the Activity	Objectives	Activity Contents	Methods and Techniques	Expected Outcomes
Understanding Values and Character	• To impart the concept of moral values • To examine the need for character development • To establish guidelines for studying moral values	• Concept of moral values • Importance of moral values • Core moral values • Sources of moral values • Concept of moral education • Understanding character	• Artistic Expression • Story Telling • Speeches	• Understanding of the need and importance of moral values
Values: Respect Acceptance Peace Honesty Humbleness Kindness Forgiveness Obedience	• To develop and understanding of the concept and essence of the value • To discuss the importance of the value • To teach how to inculcate the value	• Concept explanation • Importance of the value • Value components • Different situations	• Artistic Expression • Story Telling • Experience sharing • Examples of situations • Situation Play • Role Play • Promotional Quote	• Inculcation of the respective moral values in students

Name of the Activity	Objectives	Activity Contents	Methods and Techniques	Expected Outcomes
Patience Responsibility Sincerity				
Conclusion	• To summarize the discussed moral values • To procure feedback • To close effectively and impactfully	• Summary of the values • Experience sharing • Feedback	• Artistic Expression • Speech • Lesson Sharing	• Impactful deliverance of moral values

Total No. of Activities: 41

INTRODUCTORY SESSION: VALUES AND CHARACTER

2

INTRODUCTORY SESSION: VALUES AND CHARACTER

2.1 DEFINITIONS

- **Moral Value** – A moral value is a universally accepted ethical principle that governs the day-to-day living of life.
- **Character** – The complex of mental and ethical traits marking a person.

2.2 SESSION OBJECTIVES

- To impart the concept of moral values.
- To examine the need for character development.
- To establish guidelines for studying moral values.

2.3 SESSION OUTLINE

Activity No.	Activity Name	Duration
2.3.1	Preliminary Discussion	20 minutes
2.3.2	Good Behaviour, Bad Behaviour	20 minutes
2.3.3	Positive Values, Negative Values	20 minutes
	Total Time	**1 hour**

2.3.1 Preliminary Discussion

(a) Material Required: Discussion Points.

(b) Instructions: Tell the class that we are going to initiate lessons on 'VALUES AND CHARACTER'. Write the term 'Values' and 'Character' on the board and facilitate a brief discussion around the following discussion points and their broad responses as should be expected:

(i) **What do we mean by 'moral values'?**—Moral values are good and positive attributes and attitudes. Moral values are usually communal and shared by the public in general. Some examples of moral values are patience, generosity, kindness, and compassion.

(ii) **What do we mean by character?**—Character refers to the stable and distinctive qualities of a person, which determine his/her response to different situations, regardless of the circumstances. For example, a truthful person will more likely tell the truth about a bad incident to the educator; an alert person will more likely be a better driver; a tolerant person will more readily accept others who are different than him/her etc.

Character can be good or bad. When we say that someone has character, or good character, it usually means that they are honourable, honest, respectful, responsible etc. However, when we say that someone has a bad character, it usually means that they are not trustworthy, responsible, truthful etc.

(iii) **Why should we have good moral values / good character?—**

Having good moral values and good character is important for several reasons:

- Good values and character help us to achieve success.
- Good values and character affect the quality of our lives.
- Good values and character help in maintaining unity and harmony between people.
- Good values and character help us to feel good about ourselves.

(iv) What are some of the core moral values?—There are many moral values that are shared by people all-around the world. Some of the significant ones are:

- Respect
- Acceptance
- Peace
- Honesty
- Humility
- Kindness
- Forgiveness
- Obedience
- Patience
- Responsibility
- Sincerity

2.3.2 Good Behaviour, Bad Behaviour

(a) Material Required: None.

(b) Instructions: Tell the class that we are going to play a very simple and fun game. Tell them that you are going to announce certain behaviours/actions, and the whole class has to ascertain whether it is a good behaviour/action or a bad behaviour/action. Instruct them, however, that they have to answer in silence and only in action, i.e. if they think it is a good behaviour/action to do, then they must stand, but if they think that it is a bad behaviour/action to do, then they must sit. Give an example or two, to make the instructions clear – such as, if you say "speaking the truth", then they must stand quickly, but if you say "lying to someone", then they should sit down immediately.

Use the following behaviours/actions among any other that you may think of:

- Hitting someone
- Speaking the truth
- Lying to someone
- Stealing your friend's lunch
- Obeying your educator
- Stealing your partner's pencils
- Kicking a dog
- Helping your mother
- Shouting in class
- Pulling someone's hair
- Fighting with a classmate
- Finishing your homework
- Hugging your grandmother
- Complaining to the educator
- Skipping school

Make sure that the children are identifying good behaviours from bad behaviours correctly. If you have time, you may call on volunteers to come to the front of the class and speak good and bad behaviours, while the others continue to follow the instructions of the game.

Appreciate the class for learning the difference between good behaviours and bad behaviours.

2.3.3 Positive Values, Negative Values

(a) Material Required: None.

(b) Instructions: Follow up from the previous activity, and tell the class that they are now going to move from learning good behaviours to learning positive and negative values. Tell them that it is important to differentiate between behaviours and values, because we can see the behaviours or the actions, but we can't see the values. Remind the students that our behaviours are in fact determined by the values we have inside us.

Now, pick up the following situations one by one, and ask the class to assess why the particular behaviour is bad. Provide them with a context in which the action can be termed bad. Seek responses on the negative value that the person could have (such as irresponsibility, dishonesty etc.). After this, use the same value to change the context in which it is done, so that it becomes a valued action. Ask the children if the action was bad in the given context. Help them identify the different (positive) values that is possessed by the doer in the given situation.

Use the following table for examples, and feel free to add more:

Action	Done with Negative Value	Done with Positive Value
Lying to someone	My friend came to my house to play with me, and forgot to tell her mother about it. Her mother got very worried and started looking for her in the neighbourhood. When her mother reached my house, I felt scared that the mother will take my friend away with her. So I lied to her and said that her daughter is not at my house. I closed the door and went back to play with my friend.	My friend gets really badly beaten up at home. She came to my house one day, because she wanted help from my parents. I knew my parents could help in a good way, so I took her in. Her mother started looking for her, so that she could beat her more. When she came to my house, I got scared that my bruised friend will be beaten up even more. So I lied, saying that her daughter is not at my house. I felt very bad, but planned to apologize later, after the matter had been brought to my parents' notice.
Hitting someone	I was walking around my neighbourhood, and saw a little boy playing with his toy. I really wanted that toy, so I hit him and snatched the toy, before running away from there.	I was walking around my neighbourhood and I saw a group of boys of my age hitting a smaller and younger boy from my school. I ran towards them and tried to talk to them, but they were

Action	Done with Negative Value	Done with Positive Value
		too busy in beating up the little boy, and did not pay attention to me. To save the little boy, I eventually pushed the big boy off of him and controlled him with physical force, before I could reason with him.
Skipping school	I skipped school for 1 week because I wanted to stay at home and watch TV. I enjoyed a lot!	I skipped school for 1 week because I got really sick and the fever remained for a whole week. I felt very bad about missing school!
Complaining to the educator	My friend forgot to bring his notebook, so I complained to the educator in front of the whole class. We all laughed as he was being scolded.	My friend kept on bullying me and saying that if I didn't give him my new pencil box, then he will hurt me very bad. I didn't want to do it, but I had to complain to the educator.

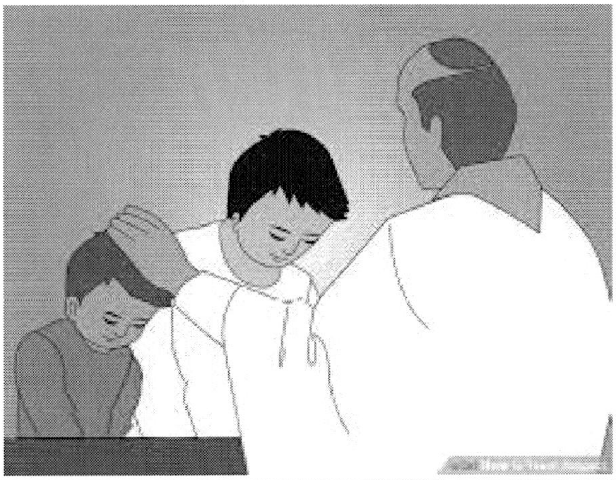

RESPECT

SESSION 3
RESPECT

3.1 DEFINITION

Respecting someone means you act in a way that shows you care about their feelings and well-being. You can have respect for others, and for yourself.

3.2 SESSION OBJECTIVES

- To develop an understanding of the concept and essence of the value of respect.
- To discuss the importance of the value of respect.
- To inculcate the value of respect in children.

3.3 SESSION OUTLINE

Activity No.	Activity Name	Duration
3.3.1	Preliminary Discussion	20 minutes
3.3.2	Quiz	20 minutes
3.3.3	Chart of Respect	40 minutes
	Total Time	**1 hour 20 minutes**

3.3.1 Preliminary Discussion

(a) Material Required: Discussion Points.

(b) Instructions: Tell the class that the topic of the day / the week is 'RESPECT'. Write the term 'Respect' on the board and facilitate a brief discussion around the following discussion points and their broad responses as should be expected:

(i) **What do we mean by 'respect'?**—Respect means a lot of different things. On a practical level, it includes taking someone's feelings, needs, thoughts, ideas, wishes and preferences into consideration. When the feeling is there, the behaviour will naturally follow.

For example, if a baby needs to be fed at three in the morning we don't do it begrudgingly if we respect his natural needs; we simply accept that the infant has a natural need to eat at that particular moment. Likewise, if a children or an adult needs to talk, we accept this need and we show respect by listening voluntarily.

(ii) **Why should we show respect?**—We should show respect to avoid hurting other people or things. In that way, we can promote peace and happiness.

(iii) **How can we show respect?**—Respect can be shown in multiple ways, depending on the context. Some examples of showing respect include:

- Listening to those we want to respect
- Keeping unkind thoughts to ourselves
- Speaking kindly
- Playing fairly and waiting for our turn

- Saying "please" and "thank you"
- Raising our hand before talking
- Cleaning up after ourselves
- Obeying rules
- Not hitting or hurting anyone with our words
- Sharing

(iv) Who all should we respect?—We should respect everyone around us without any discrimination about who he/she is or where he/she comes from. We should also respect things of any value to anyone. In simple terms, we should respect:

- Our elders
- Our peers
- Those who are younger to us
- Animals
- Our educators
- Our school
- Our community and other communities
- Our country and other countries
- Ourselves
- Rules
- Property
- Differences
- Environment

3.3.2 Quiz

(a) Material Required: Quiz Questions.

(b) Instructions: Divide the class into four or five groups (this could be done easily as per their seating arrangement in class; for example, those sitting in one row of furniture could form one team). Simply number or name the teams (as 1, 2, 3, 4.... or A, B, C, D....) and make a scorecard on the blackboard. Now tell the class that they are going to play a parallel quiz on the topic of 'respect'. Give the following instructions / rules for playing the quiz:

- The quiz is based on the preliminary discussion had with the class.
- There will be one question for each round.
- Each question will have multiple answers.
- Each team should give one answer each for every question to gain one point.
- Students of the teams should raise their hand if they know the answer.
- Students should answer only when asked by the educator.
- If any team speaks without their turn (without being asked or in some other team's turn), then they will lose two points for showing disrespect to rules and to others.

Assure the students that you will give equal opportunity to all the teams to answer first. Now start the quiz and include the following questions:

- Why is it important to show respect?
- Who all should we respect?
- What are the benefits of showing respect?
- Give an example of respectful behaviour.
- Why is it important to respect our family?

Total up the points as per the given rules and instructions. Make the class clap for the team that wins and make the winning team the respect ambassador of the class.

3.3.3 Chart of Respect

(a) Material Required

- Chart
- Coloured A4 size sheets
- Black Marker
- Sketch Pens

(b) Instructions: Divide the class into four groups. Give each group one coloured A4 size sheet with the following headings written in advance:

(i) We like to be treated in the following ways
(ii) We don't like to be treated in the following ways
(iii) We should respect all of the following
(iv) Respect is important because

Instruct the groups to work together to list down as many things as they can under the given heading. Tell them that they have 20 minutes to do this and that they should try to do it as neatly as possible because it will be put on a chart for the class bulletin board. As the groups complete their listings, help them to stick their coloured sheets on the common chart retained by you. Once the chart has all the four sheets stuck, discuss the listings in class and add any point that the groups may have missed. Put up the chart on the class bulletin board for children to regularly encounter.

3.4 FOLLOW UP

1. Make the children watch a cartoon or a short film, and then discuss about how the actions of the characters demonstrated either respectful or disrespectful behaviour. Share storey on Respect (Annexure 1A).
2. Ask the children to write or speak about a time when they were disrespectful to someone. Why did it happen? Was it the right thing to do? What were the consequences? How did it make the other person feel? What did they learn from the experience?

Annexure 1A

Value: Respect Activity: Story

THE WOODEN BOWL

A frail old man went to live with his son, daughter-in-law, and four year old grandson. The old man's hands trembled, his eyesight was blurred, and his steps faltered. One good practice in the family was that the family always ate dinner together at the dinning table. But the elderly grandfather's shaky hands and failing sight made eating difficult. Generally peas, rolled off his spoon on to the floor. When he grasped the glass, milk spilled on the tablecloth.

The son and daughter-in-law became irritated with the regular mess. Feeling embarrassed, one day the son said "we must do something about father," said the son. "I have had enough of his spilled milk, noisy eating, and food on the floor." So, the husband and wife set a small table in the corner. There, Grandfather ate alone while the rest of the family continued to eat dinner together. Since Grandfather had broken a dish or two, his food was also served in a wooden thali and a bowl! When the family glanced in Grandfather's direction, sometimes a small tear was visible which always went unnoticed by the family members. Still, the only expressions the couple had for him were sharp admonitions when he dropped a fork or spilled food.

All this while, the four year old was a lone spectator.

One evening before supper, the father noticed his son playing with wood scraps on the floor. He asked the child sweetly, "What are you making?" Just as sweetly and innocently came the reply "Oh, I am making a little bowl for you and Mama to eat your food in when I grow up." The four year old smiled and went back to work.

The words struck the parents sharp and they turned speechless. It was only then that the father realized his mistake and tears rolled down his cheeks.Though no word was spoken, but both the parents of that little boy knew what must be done.

That evening the husband took Grandfather's hand and gently led him back to the old dining table. For the remainder of his life, he ate every meal with the family. The husband and wife thereafter did not care any longer when a fork was dropped, or the milk was spilled, or the tablecloth soiled.

Moral: Always respect, care and love your parents unconditionally.

Source: https://www.moralstories.org/the-wooden-bowl/

ACCEPTANCE

SESSION 4
ACCEPTANCE

4.1 DEFINITION

The act of accepting – of receiving what is offered, with good opinion, satisfaction, or consent. It means to especially give a favourable response and/or approval of what you have or have been given.

4.2 SESSION OBJECTIVES

- To develop an understanding of the concept and essence of the value of acceptance.
- To discuss the importance of the value of acceptance.
- To inculcate the value of acceptance in children.

4.3 SESSION OUTLINE

Activity No.	Activity Name	Duration
4.3.1	Preliminary Discussion	15 minutes
4.3.2	Accepting our Neighbours	30 minutes
4.3.3	The Me Tree	1 hour
	Total Time	**1 hour 45 minutes**

4.3.1 Preliminary Discussion

(a) Material Required: Discussion Points.

(b) Instructions: Tell the class that the topic of the day / the week is 'ACCEPTANCE'. Write the term 'Acceptance' on the board and facilitate a brief discussion around the following discussion points and their broad responses as should be expected:

(i) **What do we mean by 'acceptance'?**—Everyone we know is unique in their own way.

They have somethings that we don't have, and they don't have some things that we have. For example, we may have both mother and father, but some children don't have a father or don't have a mother. It is just their exceptional circumstance.

Acceptance means to accept these differences, about us also and about others also. It means to not judge, or call names, or tease someone about their particular characteristics.

(ii) Why should we show acceptance?—If somebody teases us about something we don't have, then we feel bad. For example, if I am not tall, I may be called names likes *"thiggu", "bauna"* etc. This will not make me feel nice and I will feel very bad about myself. Therefore, it is very important to protect myself from feeling bad, because I cannot change my height on my own.

In the same way, our friends may not have everything that we have. Therefore, to protect their feelings from being hurt, we should learn to accept them as they are, without any judgement or bad response.

(iii) How can we demonstrate acceptance?—Acceptance can be demonstrated in various ways, depending upon the context. Consider the following situations and how acceptance can be demonstrated in them.

- A new student came to school who was twice the size of everyone in the class, yet he was the same age as everyone else. What will you do to show acceptance? Will you ignore him, or point at him and laugh, or call him names? Or will you treat him like everybody else?
- I cannot afford to buy new nice clothes. In order to feel accepted, should I have to steal clothes, or borrow clothes from others, or stay back at home only? Or should I be carefree about clothes and just go play with my friends?

- Because of an illness, a girl is overweight and does not participate in sports. What should other students in class do to accept her condition? Should they pick on her and call her names? Should they avoid talking to her? Should they tease her about her weight? Or should they only focus on her strengths?
- One boy is differently abled and has to use crutches/ wheelchair for moving around the school. How can the other students show acceptance of his circumstances? Should they open doors for him? Should they clear pathways when he needs to get through? Should they treat him like everyone else? Or should they ignore him and call him names?

Similarly, you can think of other situations and how acceptance can be demonstrated in them.

4.3.2 Accepting Our Neighbours

(a) Material Required: None.

(b) Instructions: Tell the children that we will start by learning to accept our neighbours – our partners in the context of class. Explain to the children that they will get five minutes to talk to their partners, in which they have to find out two things:

- one thing that their partner is good at doing – that he/she can help them with.
- one thing that their partner is not good at doing – that he/she needs help with.

In the same vein, they should also give their partners the same information about themselves. Give clues to children that the answers could relate to study subjects (that they are good at or not good at), games (that they are good at or not good at), attributes (that they are good at or not good at) like talking in class, talking to others, problem-solving etc.

After five minutes, make the pairs tell the class what they found out, and make them each say "I accept my partner".

4.3.3 The 'Me' Tree

(a) Material Required:

(i) Drawing sheets for all children
(ii) Pencils for all children
(iii) Crayons for all children
(iv) Cuts outs of leaves in green paper for all children
(v) Cut outs of leaves in yellow paper for all children
(vi) Sticking Glue

(b) Instructions: Tell the children that this activity is about accepting ourselves. Distribute drawing sheets and instruct children to draw a big sized tree on their respective sheets. Distribute pencils and crayons for the same.

Once the children have drawn their simple trees and coloured them, give out two cut outs of yellow leaves and two cut outs of green leaves each to every child. Now tell the children that the yellow leaves signify their shortcomings or weaknesses and the green leaves signify their strong points and strengths. Thinking of themselves likewise, the children must write two things—they are not good at doing on the two yellow leaves, and two things that they are good at doing on the two green leaves. After this, they must stick their yellow leaves and green leaves on their trees, to complete their acceptance trees. Assist the children in completing the task.

4.4 FOLLOW UP

1. Use things available in the daily life of school to show children the differences in people. This can be demonstrated through a short film, a book, or simply walking through the school playground where children from other classes are present.

2. Hold short discussions on the differences between people in the following aspects:
   - Differences on the basis of religion.
   - Differences on the basis of race, culture and region.
   - Differences on the basis of physical abilities.
   - Differences on the basis of sex and gender.

Teach children to accept these differences gracefully.

PEACE

SESSION 5

PEACE

5.1 DEFINITION

It is the presence of love for each other, compassion for fellow beings, humility for our mistakes, forgiveness for the errors of others and acceptance of our differences. Peace is not the mere absence of war or violence. Peace refers to a time when there is no fighting, no rudeness, no cruelty, but only calmness.

5.2 SESSION OBJECTIVES

- To develop an understanding of the concept and essence of the value of peace-keeping.
- To discuss the importance of the value of peace keeping.
- To inculcate the value of peace keeping in children.

5.3 SESSION OUTLINE

Activity no.	Activity name	Duration
5.3.1	Preliminary Discussion	10 minutes
5.3.2	Deep Breathing	10 minutes
5.3.3	Peace Tree	1 hour
5.3.4	Peace Puppets	20 minutes
Total Time		**1 hour 40 minutes**

5.3.1 Preliminary Discussion

(a) Material Required: Discussion Points

(b) Instructions: Tell the class that the topic of the day / the week is 'PEACE'. Write the term 'Peace' on the board and facilitate a brief discussion around the following discussion points and their broad responses as should be expected:

(i) **What do we mean by 'peace'?**—Peace means many things. It means:

- absence of war (freedom from war, or the time when a war or conflict ends).
- law and order (the absence of violence or other disturbances within a state).
- state of harmony (freedom from conflict or disagreement among people or groups of people).
- mental calm (a state of mental calm and serenity, with no anxiety).

(ii) **Why should we maintain peace?**—Peace is important to make the world a good and happy place for everyone. When we fight, we do not feel good. Even if sometimes we may win a fight or an argument, we end up hurting someone, or feel guilty. We especially do not like it when we lose a fight or an argument. Essentially, fights, conflicts, and wars end up causing damage to one or both sides. On the other hand, a state of harmony and mental calm makes everyone feel good and safe.

(iii) **What can we do to create peace around us?**—We can do many things to help promote and maintain peace. In a given circumstance, we can practice forgiveness, sharing, caring, positive communication, tolerance, unity in diversity, respect for all, and so much more.

5.3.2 Deep Breathing

(a) Material Required: None.

(b) Instructions: Instruct the children to sit in a relaxed posture with their eyes closed. Ask them to use their right hand for the instructions that will follow and to concentrate on breathing. Then slowly instruct them to close their right nostril with their thumb (of their right hand) and inhale with the left nostril. Now ask them to close their left nostril with their ring finger and little finger (while leave their thumb lose) and exhale with the right nostril. Ask them to inhale again with the right nostril. Close the right nostril and exhale with the left nostril. This is one cycle. Tell them to think that with every breath that we take in, we are becoming calm and quiet; and that with every breath we take out, we are removing our anger.

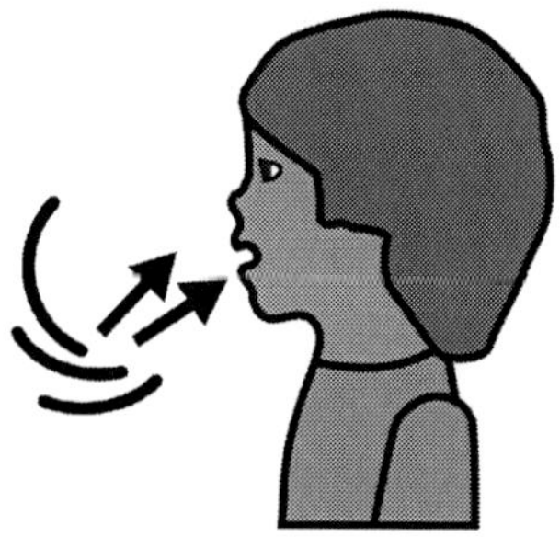

Repeat the cycle about 15 to 20 times.

5.3.3 Peace Tree

(a) Material Required:

(i) Paper Cardboard

(ii) Green Paper

(iii) Scissors

(iv) Sticking Glue

(b) Instructions: Before going to class, prepare two things:

- a paper cardboard cut in the shape of a tree.
- cut outs of leaves made from green paper (at least one leaf for each child).

Upon entering class, put the cardboard tree on the wall and write the word 'PEACE' on the class board. Distribute green leaves so that each child gets one leaf. Ask the students to close their eyes and think what comes to their mind when they hear 'PEACE'. Make them write it down on their leaf. (Tell them that it could be an incident, name of a person, their view of peace etc.) Call all children one by one to stick up their leaves on the cardboard tree and speak aloud what they have written (if they want to). Pin the leaves on the tree and create the 'PEACE TREE' for your class.

5.3.4 Peace Puppets

(a) Material Required: War and Peace Puppets.

(b) Instructions: Prepare two simple finger puppets and take them to class. Tell the class that they are going to participate in some interesting puppetry. Then execute the simple puppetry as follows:

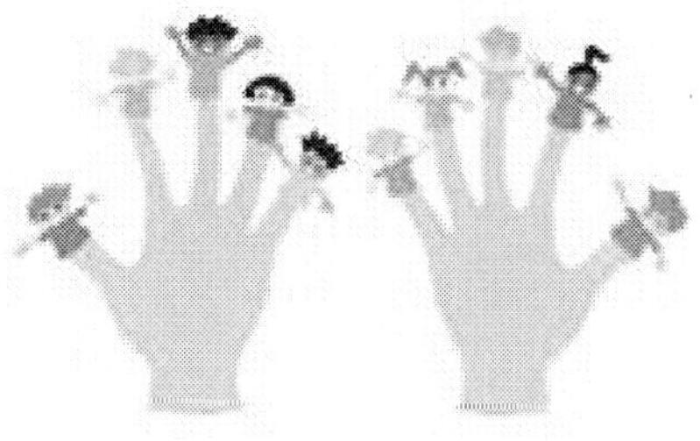

PUPPET 1: Well then! My name is *LADAKU*. I am a war puppet and I love wars.

PUPPET 2: Dear children! My name is *SHANTI*. I am a peace puppet and I am here to ask you to please help me explain my friend *Ladaku* here, the importance of peace.

PUPPET 1: I love wars as they help me get power.

PUPPET 2: Children! Is he right? (Listen to replies)

Are wars good? (Listen to replies)

What are the harms of wars? (Listen to replies)

So *Ladaku* I think you now understand that wars are bad. Never Fight.

5.4 Follow Up

1. Discuss the 'Peace Heroes' of the world with children. Tell them about the following famous people and ask them to find out more about them:
    - Mahatma Gandhi: Taught Ahimsa to the world.
    - Martin Luther King: Fought for the civil rights.
    - Mother Teresa: Lead Missionary of Charity; worked for hunger and the poor.

- 14th Dalai Lama: Fighting against violence.
- Aung San Suu Kyi: Fighting for democracy in Myanmar.
- Nelson Mandela: Fought the apartheid regime.

2. Share the peace prayers of different religions with children (Annexure 5A). After the prayers tell the students how each religion emphasizes upon the values of peace and tolerance sharing story on peace (Annexure 5B).

Annexure 5A

Value: Peace **Activity: Prayer**

PEACE PRAYERS OF THE WORLD

BAHA'I PRAYER FOR PEACE

Be generous in prosperity, and thankful in adversity.
Be fair in thy judgement, and guarded in thy speech.
Be a lamp unto those who walk in darkness, and a home to the stranger.
Be eyes to the blind, and a guiding light unto the feet of the erring.
Be a breath of life to the body of humankind,
a dew to the soil of the human heart,
and a fruit upon the tree of humility.

BUDDHIST PRAYER FOR PEACE

May all beings everywhere plagued with sufferings of body and mind quickly be freed from their illnesses.
May those frightened cease to be afraid, and may those bound be free.
May the powerless find power, and may people think of befriending one another.
May those who find themselves in trackless, fearful wildernesses—the children, the aged, the unprotected—
Be guarded by beneficent celestials, and may they swiftly attain Buddhahood.

CHRISTIAN PRAYER FOR PEACE

Blessed are the Peacemakers,
for they shall be known as the Children of God.

But I say to you that hear, love your enemies,
do good to those who hate you,
bless those who curse you,
pray for those who abuse you.

To those who strike you on the cheek, offer the other also,
and from those who take away your cloak,
do not withhold your coat as well.

Give to everyone who begs from you,
and of those who take away your goods, do not ask them again.

And as you wish that others would do to you, do so to them.

HINDU PRAYERS FOR PEACE

Oh God, lead us from the unreal to the Real.
Oh God, lead us from darkness to light.
Oh God, lead us from death to immortality.
Shanti, Shanti, Shanti unto all.

Oh Lord God almighty, may there be peace in celestial regions.
May there be peace on earth.
May the waters be appeasing.
May herbs be wholesome, and may trees and plants bring peace to all.
May all beneficent beings bring peace to us.
May thy Vedic Law propagate peace all through the world.
May all things be a source of peace to us.
And may thy peace itself, bestow peace on all,
and may that peace come to me also.

JAINIST PRAYER FOR PEACE

Peace and Universal Love is the essence of the Gospel
preached by all the Enlightened Ones.

The Lord has preached that equanimity is the Dharma.

Forgive do I creatures all, and let all creatures forgive me.

Unto all have I amity, and unto none enmity.

Know that violence is the root cause of all miseries in the world.

Violence, in fact, is the knot of bondage.

"Do not injure any living being."

This is the eternal, perennial, and unalterable way of spiritual life.

JEWISH PRAYER FOR PEACE

Come let us go up to the mountain of the Lord,
that we may walk the paths of the Most High.

And we shall beat our swords into ploughshares,
and our spears into pruning hooks.

Nation shall not lift up sword against nation—
neither shall they learn war any more.

And none shall be afraid,
for the mouth of the Lord of Hosts has spoken.

MUSLIM PRAYER FOR PEACE

In the name of Allah, the beneficent, the merciful.

Praise be to the Lord of the Universe who has created us and made us into tribes and nations, that we may know each other, not that we may despise each other.

If the enemy incline towards peace, do thou also incline towards peace, and trust in God, for the Lord is the one that heareth and knoweth all things.

And the servants of God, most gracious are those who walk on the Earth in humility, and when we address them, we say "PEACE."

SIKH PRAYER FOR PEACE

God adjudges us according to our deeds, not the coat that we wear: that Truth is above everything, but higher still is truthful living.

Know that we attaineth God when we loveth, and only that victory endures in consequence of which no one is defeated.

Know that we attain God when we love, and only that victory endures in consequence of which no one is defeated.

Annexure 5B

Value: Peace **Activity: Story**

THE REAL MEANING OF PEACE

There once was a king who offered a prize to the artist who would paint the best picture of peace. Many artists tried. The king looked at all the pictures. But there were only two he really liked, and he had to choose between them. One picture was of a calm lake. The lake was a perfect mirror for peaceful towering mountains all around it. Overhead was a blue sky with fluffy white clouds.

All who saw this picture thought that it was a perfect picture of peace.The other picture had mountains, too. But these were rugged and bare. The above was an angry sky, from which rain fell and in which lightning played. Down the side of the mountain tumbled a foaming waterfall. This did not look peaceful at all. But when the king looked closely, he saw behind the waterfall a tiny bush growing in a crack in the rock. In the bush a mother bird had built her nest. There, in the midst of the rush of angry water, sat the mother bird on her nest—in perfect peace.

Which picture do you think won the prize? The king chose the second picture. Do you know why? "Because," explained the king, "peace does not mean to be in a place where there is no noise, trouble, or hard work. Peace means to be in the midst of all those things and still be calm in your heart. That is the real meaning of peace."

Moral: Peaceful mind and heart is work in consonance.

Source: http://www.iamspiritual.com/chai/pp-e/moralstory10.html

HONESTY

SESSION 6
HONESTY

6.1 DEFINITION

Honesty means to tell the truth and have straightforward conduct. An honest person is sincere, trustworthy, honourable, fair, genuine, and loyal with integrity.

6.2 SESSION OBJECTIVES

- To develop an understanding of the concept and essence of the value of honesty.
- To discuss the importance of the value of honesty.
- To inculcate the value of honesty in children.

6.3 SESSION OUTLINE

Activity No.	Activity Name	Duration
6.3.1	Preliminary Discussion	10 minutes
6.3.2	All Those	15 minutes
6.3.3	I Share, You Share	30 minutes
6.3.4	True Lies	35 minutes
	Total Time	**1 hour 30 minutes**

6.3.1 Preliminary Discussion

(a) Material Required: Discussion Points.

(b) Instructions: Tell the class that the topic of the day / the week is 'HONESTY'. Write the term 'Honesty' on the board and facilitate a brief discussion around the following discussion points and their broad responses as should be expected:

(i) What do we mean by honesty?

A. Many children understand a definition of honesty to be "don't lie". But a complete definition of honesty also means that an honest person doesn't do things that are morally wrong. If something you do is breaking the law or you have to hide it because you'll get in trouble, you are probably not being honest.

- Honesty means you don't say things about people that aren't true. You are not being honest if you make up rumours about someone.
- Being honest means you admit to your actions, even if you'll get in trouble. You are not being honest if deny you did something wrong when you really did it.
- Honesty means you explain how a situation really happened. You are not being honest if you say something happened one way when it really happened another way.

(ii) What do honest people/children do?

Honest people / children

- Tell the truth despite consequences.
- Voice their opinion in a kind, thoughtful way.
- "Tell on" someone only when necessary.
- Show and share their feelings.
- Know their classmates and educators care and want the best for thcm.
- Feel and react without guilt.
- Express themselves positively as well as critically.

(iii) Why should we tell the truth?

There are some great reasons to tell the truth.

- Telling the truth lets everyone know what really happened. There's less chances of misunderstandings, confusion, or conflict.
- Telling the truth protects innocent people from being blamed or punished.
- Telling the truth allows everyone to learn from what happened.
- You usually get into less trouble for telling the truth than for lying (and getting caught).
- Other people trust you more when you tell the truth.
- You don't have to tell more lies to keep your story straight.
- You gain a reputation for being truthful—a trait that most people value.
- Telling the truth helps you feel secure and peaceful inside.

(iv) Why does it mean when people say "be honest with yourself"?

A big part of honesty is what you say and how you act towards others. But another part of the definition of honesty is whether you treat yourself the same way. Being honest with yourself means you really know why you are acting in a certain way or whether what you tell yourself is true.

6.3.2 All Those

(a) Material Required: None.

(b) Instructions: Tell the class that we are going to play an honesty game. Explain that in this game, you (the educator), are going to give the class some commands one by one, and the children would have to respond to them honestly. Make clear to the children that there are going to be no judgements involved in this game (give instructions to all for the same), and everyone should just answer honestly. Use the following commands for the honesty game (in addition to those you develop on your own):

(i) All those who have ever lied to their mother, stand up.
(ii) All those who have ever not done their home work, stand up.
(iii) All those who have ever stolen someone's toffee / chocolate, stand up.
(iv) All those who have ever hit someone, stand up.
(v) All those who have have ever skipped school without any good reason, stand up.
(vi) All those who who don't like to study, stand up.
(vii) All those who have ever eaten somebody else's tiffin, stand up.

6.3.3 Share, You Share

(a) Material Required: None.

(b) Instructions: Tell the class that this is a story telling activity about honesty. Talk to the class about how everyone has some certain honesty story, because we all often get thoughts about whether we should speak the truth or get away with lying. Describe how this doesn't have to mean that we all always make the right decision and act honest, but may have even been dishonest but realize later that what we did was wrong. Tell them that the most important thing is to realize our mistake and learn our lesson.

Tell the class that we will share our honesty stories with each other through this activity, so that we all can learn from each others' experiences and learn to become honest. Start with sharing your honesty story (this could be any little thing from your past that the children may relate to – whether you acted honestly or were dishonest and learnt from your mistake). Then encourage the children to volunteer to share their stories. Make sure to not force children to share but try to encourage them, by sharing more than one story of yours, if it helps. Appreciate every story shared and reiterate on the lesson learnt from it.

6.3.4 True Lies

(a) Material Required: None.

(b) Instructions: Tell the class that we will now play a fun game. Tell them that one of us will come forward and tell the others 3 things about themselves – two out of these three things should be true and one should be false. The rest of the class will have to guess which one is false. You (the educator) can begin so that the children understand the game and feel confident. Play as many rounds as possible. Encourage children to volunteer and come forward.

6.4 FOLLOW UP

1. Share simple stories of honesty with children. (Annexure 6A). Make sure to reiterate on the moral of the story.
2. Ask the students to prepare short skits on the theme of 'Honesty is the best policy'. Help them perform their skits in class, or in the school assembly.

Annexure 6A

Value: Honesty Activity: Story

THE WOODCUTTER AND THE AXE

Long ago, there lived a woodcutter in a small village. He was sincere in his work and very honest. Every day, he set out into the nearby forest to cut trees. He brought the woods back into the village and sold them out to a merchant and earn his living. He earned just about enough to make a living, but he was always satisfied with his simple living.

One day, while cutting a tree near a river, his axe slipped out of his hand and fell into the river. The river was so deep, that he could not even think to retrieve it on his own. He only had one axe which was submerged into the river. He became very much worried thinking how he will be able to earn his living now? He felt so helpless and upset that he started crying and praying to God. His sincere and true prayers moved the God. The God appeared in front of him and asked him softly, "My son ! What is your problem? Tell me." The woodcutter explained the problem with tears in his eyes and requested God to get back his axe.

God put his hand deep into the river and took out a silver axe and asked, "Is this your axe?" The Woodcutter looked at the axe and said "No". So, the God put his hand back deep into the water again and showed a golden axe and asked, "Is this your axe?" The woodcutter looked at the axe and said "No". The God said, "Take a look again Son, this is a very valuable golden axe. Are you sure this is not yours?" "No, It's not mine" came the innocent reply by the honest woodcutter.

The God smiled and finally put his hand into the water again and took out his iron axe and asked, "Is this your axe?" Seeing his axe, the woodcutter smiled wiping his tears and replied happily with joy, "Yes!

This is mine! Thank you!" The Goddess was very much impressed with his honesty and gave him his iron axe and also other two axes as a reward for his honesty. God has his own ways to reward us when we are honest.

Moral: Always be Honest. Honesty is always rewarded.

Source: https://www.moralstories.org/the-woodcutter-and-the-axe/

HUMILITY

SESSION 7

HUMILITY

7.1 DEFINITION

Humility is also called 'humbleness' sometimes. It is the quality of being meek and modest in behaviour, attitude or spirit. It means to not be arrogant or prideful.

7.2 SESSION OBJECTIVES

- To develop an understanding of the concept and essence of the value of humbleness.
- To discuss the importance of the value of humbleness.
- To inculcate the value of humbleness in children.

7.3 SESSION OUTLINE

Activity No.	Activity name	Duration
7.3.1	Preliminary Discussion	15 minutes
7.3.2	Stories of Humility	30 minutes
7.3.3	Role Playing	40 minutes
7.3.4	Mr. Arrogant & Mr. Humble	20 minutes
	Total Time	**1 hour 45 minutes**

7.3.1 Preliminary Discussion

(a) Material Required: Discussion Points.

(b) Instructions: Tell the class that the topic of the day / the week is 'HUMILITY/HUMBLENESS'. Write the term 'Humility/Humbleness' on the board and facilitate a brief discussion around the following discussion points and their broad responses as should be expected:

- **(i) What do we mean by humility?**—Humility is a modest quality. It is the opposite of arrogance, pride and vanity. Humble people do not think that they are the best; they do not have their noses high in air. Humble people take pleasure in their achievements, but not pride in them. They recognize that everyone has good qualities and appreciate everyone's achievements.
- **(ii) Why should we be humble?**—One of the many benefits of being humble is that it improves your interactions with others. People enjoy being around those who are considerate and who think about others and not just themselves. Doing this takes humility and esteeming others more important than one's self.

  On the other hand, people seldom feel comfortable around those who are so proud and self-centred that they often brag about how they can do things better than others. It's difficult to be around someone who can't lose gracefully or finds it hard to admit that he doesn't know everything.

  A person is generally happier and has more friends when he has learned to walk in humility and to admit when he needs help from others.

  Humility also engenders respect for others. It further promotes trust and peace.
- **(iii) How can we be humble?**—To be humble, you must (i) accept your limitations, and (ii) appreciate others. These two aspects can be demonstrated as follows:

- Accept your limitations—
  - Admit that you're not the best at everything – or anything.
  - Recognize your own faults.
  - Be grateful for what you have.
  - Don't be afraid to make mistakes.
  - When you do make mistakes, admit to them.
  - Avoid bragging.
  - Do not take all the credit.
- Appreciate others—
  - Appreciate the talent and qualities of others.
  - Stop comparing yourself to others.
  - Help others.
  - Go last.
  - Compliment others.
  - Apologize.
  - Listen more than you talk.

7.3.2 Stories of Humility

(a) Material Required: Humility-themed Stories.

(b) Instructions: Tell the class that you are going to share some interesting short stories with them. Tell them that the stories are going to have a moral lesson at the end, and if they listen carefully, they will be able to figure the moral of the story. In an interesting manner, read out the humility-themed stories to the class (Annexure 7A and Annexure 7B for stories). Encourage them to share what they learnt from the story, and reiterate on the lesson of humility.

7.3.3 Role Playing

(a) Material Required: None.

(b) Instructions: Call out eight volunteers to do brief role playing in front of the class. Outside the classroom, pair the volunteers to make different teams. Give each pair a situation from the following:

- Two partners are playing hand wrestling. One of them wins and then acts arrogant about it.
- Two partners just received their report cards. One of them got the first rank in class, and the other one got the tenth rank in class. The first rank holder acts arrogant about it.
- One partner wins a gold medal for winning a race. He/she acts humble with his/her friend.
- One partner gets a treat in his lunch box (put by his/her mother), while the other gets very plain food. He/she acts humble and shares the treat with his/her partner.

Ask the volunteers to prepare short skits on the situations assigned to them, and give them 5 minutes to get ready. In the meantime, settle the rest of the class and tell them that they are going to watch some short skits, and they should watch them carefully as their will be a class discussion afterwards.

Ask the volunteer pairs to enact their role plays one-by-one. Follow this up with a discussion about arrogance *versus* humility.

7.3.4 Mr. Arrogant & Mr. Humble

(a) Material Required: None.

(b) Instructions: On the blackboard, draw a stick figure or outline of a person. Label the figure Mr. or Miss Arrogant. Draw on clothing or accessories to represent arrogance, such as a crown, a foam finger saying "I'm #1" or a shirt that says "I Am Cool" Draw thought bubbles around the figure and fill them with suggestions from children about what an arrogant person would say. Children may include phrases such as "I won!" After a pause, ask the children if they like Mr. or Miss Arrogant.

On the other side of the blackboard, draw a stick figure or outline of another person. Label this figure Mr. or Miss Humble. Draw on clothing or accessories to represent humility – no fancy jewellery, simple shirt that says "Everyone is Good" or "I make mistakes but I learn from them", simple shoes and socks etc. Draw thought bubbles around the figure and fill them with suggestions from children about what a humble person would say. After a pause, ask the children if they like Mr. or Miss Humble, and compare it with Mr. or Miss Arrogant.

Reiterate on the value of humility.

7.4 FOLLOW UP

1. Remind the students that there are many people who perform thankless jobs that make our lives easier. This could be our parents, janitors in school, school librarian etc. Help them identify these people who do thankless jobs. Next, ask them to take the time to thank these people over the course of the next few days, and share what happened.
2. Ask the students to think about the humble people they know, and write a short paragraph on how they saw their humility. Examples could be how a friend did not brag about his parents' affluence, or a cousin who shared his/her new toys with them etc.

Annexure 7A

Value: Humility **Activity: Story**

THE PEACOCK AND THE CRANE

A peacock was extremely proud of his looks. He would admire his own beauty in front of other birds. He would boastfully say: "Look at me! How beautiful are my feathers and tail. I'm the most beautiful bird in this world."

The proud peacock would dance merrily spreading his long colourful features.

One day, he went near the forest lake. There he met a crane. Seeing the crane, the peacock mocked at him, "What colourless feathers you have! You look so ordinary."

The Crane replied very humbly: "Of course your feathers are colourful, bright and beautiful. But with your feathers, you cannot fly high up. However, my colourless, plain feathers helps me to fly to the zenith and can see the beauty of the nature whereas you remain live down here".

Moral of the story: Never be arrogant.

Source: https://www.essayforkids.com/the-peacock-and-the-crane-story-with-moral-in-english/

Annexure 7B

Value: Humility **Activity: Story**

THE OAK TREE AND THE REEDS

On the bank of a river grew a tall Oak tree. It stood with its roots firmly in the ground, and its head high in the air, and said to itself: "How strong I am! Nothing shall make me bow. I look down upon all other trees."

But one day there was a storm. The terrible unseen wind came and struck the proud Oak. Crash! went the trunk, down came all the beautiful branches, and the tree fell into the river. As the water carried it away, it passed a Reed that grew on the bank. The little Reed stood up tall and slender, and looked at the poor broken tree.

"O Reed," said the Tree, "how did it happen that you were not broken down and spoiled when the wind came? You are so little and weak, whereas I was so strong and sturdy".

"Ah, Dearr Tree!" said the Reed, "that is just the reason that the wind did not hurt me. I bent low until it had gone by, but you stood stiff and tried to stop it on its way. No one can stop the wind. It must go where it is sent, but it will not hurt those who are not proud and stubborn and ready to bend when required."

Moral of the story: Pride makes you fall.

Source: https://www.essayforkids.com/the-oak-tree-and-the-reeds-english-story-with-moral-for-kids/

KINDNESS

SESSION 8
KINDNESS

8.1 DEFINITION

Kindness is the act or the state of being kind. It is marked by charitable behaviour, pleasantness, tenderness and concern for others.

8.2 SESSION OBJECTIVE

- To develop an understanding of the concept and essence of the value of kindness.
- To discuss the importance of the value of kindness.
- To inculcate the value of kindness in children.

8.3 SESSION OUTLINE

Activity No.	Activity Name	Duration
8.3.1	Preliminary Discussion	10 minutes
8.3.2	Torn Heart Game	40 minutes
8.3.3	Stories of Kindness	40 minutes
	Total Time	**1 hour 30 minutes**

8.3.1 Preliminary Discussion

(a) Material Required: Discussion Points.

(b) Instructions: Tell the class that the topic of the day / the week is 'KINDNESS'. Write the term 'Kindness' on the board and facilitate a brief discussion around the following discussion points and their broad responses as should be expected:

(i) What do we mean by kindness?

Kindness is concern about the well-being and feelings of others. Kind people are tender, considerate and helpful in nature.

(ii) Why should we be kind?

There are many reasons for being kind. Some of them are written below:

- Being kind feels good
- All religions encourage kindness
- Kindness broadens our perspective
- Kindness softens our heart
- Kindness brightens our world
- Kindness helps people feel respected and less alone
- Kindness makes people want to be around us
- Kindness bears wonderful fruit
- Kindness begets kindness

(iii) How can we show kindness?

There are many ways in which you can show kindness to the world. Most of the time, it depends on what the situation demands. Here are some ways to show kindness:

- Smile
- Listen
- Volunteer
- Be a real friend
- Encourage others
- Include someone new
- Give a compliment

- Respect others
- Show concern
- Teach a skill
- Be genuine
- Forgive
- Share

8.3.2 Torn Heart Game

(a) Material Required:

(i) Paper cardboard cut out in the shape of a heart.

(ii) Pens, pencils and erasers for children.

(iii) Tape.

(b) Instructions: Show the class the heart-shaped paper cardboard. Tell the children that you are going to pass this card around and the children can make any small cut or mark on it. Let each child get a chance to make such a cut or mark. When all children have done so, take the heart shaped cardboard and pass it around again. This time, tell the kids to fix the damage that has been done to the heart. Tell them to use erasers, tapes, or any other item to fix the damage, and make it look good again. After the game, talk to the class about how even though they tried to repair the heart, it still shows signs of damage. Explain to them how hard it is to repair the damage once hurt has been caused, and therefore, why it is important to be kind.

8.3.3 Stories of Kindness

(a) Material Required: Kindness-themed Stories.

(b) Instructions: Tell the class that you are going to share some interesting short stories with them. Tell them that the stories are going to have a moral lesson at the end, and if they listen carefully, they will be able to figure the moral of the story. In an interesting manner, read out the kindness-themed stories to the class (Annexure 8A, Annexure 8B and Annexure 8C for stories). Encourage them to share what they learnt from the story, and reiterate on the lesson of kindness.

8.4 FOLLOW UP

1. Conduct a situation play / discussion / writing exercise with children. Provide them with different situations, and seek their answers on how they will show kindness in the given situation. You may consider some of the following situations, or create your own by class/school experience.
2. Use Annexure 8D to provide children worksheets, in which they can play word search of words and terms related to kindness.

Annexure 8A

Value: Kindness **Activity: Story**

TURNING FEAR INTO TRUE COMPASSION

A girl, called Rekha used to maintain an exercise regime that included brisk walk every morning around some gardens in her neighbourhood. One morning, she was walking little early than usual, it was still relatively dark.

As she was walking, a cyclist came up to her, snatched her handbag (containing her keys, phone and credit cards) and sped off with it! She ran after him shouting "thief - thief". A man further ahead must have heard her, or seen what had happened. He was washing a car and had a bucket of water with him. He grabbed the bucket and threw the water on to the cyclist.

The cyclist, caught off guard, drove off the pavement and his bike fell over. The other people in the park rushed over and surrounded him. Rekha was worried that the people would try and beat him up, and so, she pleaded with them not to hurt him.

She bent down and asked the man why he did this to her? He was extremely repentant and explained that he was the son of a poor farmer and that this year their crops had failed. He said that the money lenders had threatened to beat up his father and hurt their family if they didn't pay on time. He said that he was absolutely desperate and didn't know what else to do. He was very sorry.

Rekha was deeply moved by this story. She could see that boy was young and he was so skinny and bony. She looked into the boy's eyes and said that she forgave him. She then pulled out some money from her handbag and gave it to him. She told him that stealing was wrong and that he shouldn't do it again. He promised and said he will not repeat it again.

Moral: Have patience and be kind.

Source: http://www.kindspring.org/story/view.php?sid=18799

Annexure 8B

Value: Kindness Activity: Story

ABRAHAM LINCOLN

When Abraham Lincoln became the president of America, his father was a shoemaker. And, naturally, egoistic people were very much offended that a shoemaker's son should become the president. They were aristocrats, who thought it was their birthright to be in the highest government post. A shoemaker's son? On the first day, as Abraham Lincoln entered to give his inaugural address, just in the middle, one man stood up. He was a very rich aristocrat. He said, "Mr. Lincoln, you should not forget that your father used to make shoes for my family." And the whole Senate laughed; they thought that they had made a fool of Abraham Lincoln.

But Lincoln – and that type of person is made of a totally different mettle – Lincoln looked at the man and said, "Sir, I know that my father used to make shoes in your house for your family, and there will be many others here... because the way he made shoes, nobody else could. He was a creator. His shoes were not just shoes, he poured his whole soul in it. I want to ask you, have you any complaint? Because I know how to make shoes myself; if you have any complaint I can make another pair of shoes. But as far as I know, nobody has ever complained about my father's shoes. He was a genius, a creator, and I am proud of my father!"

The whole Senate was struck dumb. They could not understand what kind of man Abraham Lincoln was. He had made shoe-making an art, a creativity. And he was proud because his father did the job so well that not even a single complaint had ever been heard. And even though he was the president of America, he was ready to make another pair if there was any complaint. The man looked silly and felt ashamed of what he said.

Moral: It does not matter what you do, be Kind and polite in using words.

Source: http://www.movemequotes.com/abraham-lincoln-son-shoemaker/

Annexure 8C

Value: Kindness **Activity: Story**

GAUTAM BUDDHA AND SWAN

Gautam Buddha, the founder of Buddhism, was born in 563 BCE in the kingdom of Kapilavastu, located probably in what is now Nepal. His parents, King Sudhodhana and Queen Maya, named him Siddhartha.

More than two thousand five hundred years ago, the Sakya king Sudhodhana ruled over the kingdom of Kapilavastu, on the borders of what is now Nepal. King Sudhodhana and his queen, Maya, had no children.

One night, as Queen Maya lay sleeping, she had a strange dream. She dreamt that a beautiful baby elephant, as white as snow, came down from the sky and entered her body. At once, music began to play, trees and bushes blossomed with flowers, and lotuses covered the lakes. The whole world began to celebrate.

The next morning, the queen described her strange dream. The Brahmin priests foretold that soon a son would be born to her, a son who would become either a great king or a great sage. A few months later, the queen gave birth to a beautiful baby boy. King Sudhodhana and Queen Maya named their son Siddhartha.

The king and queen surrounded their son with every luxury and comfort that they could think of. Siddhartha's days were spent in the palace and its beautiful gardens, playing and learning with his cousins, friends and companions. His best friends were his cousin Ananda, his squire Chandak and his horse Kantak.

Siddhartha was a kind and gentle child, and everyone who met him loved him, except his cousin Devadatta. Devadatta hated Siddhartha. He hated his kind nature and his innate compassion. He also hated him because of the fact that he was loved so dearly by everyone in the palace. Devadatta used every opportunity he could get to pick a fight with Siddhartha, or to create trouble for him.

One lovely spring morning, Siddhartha was playing by the river that flowed through the palace gardens. He saw a group of swans floating gracefully on the river. Siddhartha stopped to watch them. The great white birds swam slowly down the river, their feathers edged with gold in the bright sunshine. "Oh, you're beautiful," whispered Siddhartha to the swans. Siddhartha sat down by the riverbank to watch the birds.

Suddenly an arrow came whizzing out of the air, and pierced the biggest, most beautiful of the swans. Siddhartha cried out, and ran into the river towards the bird. The poor swan was thrashing his wings in fear and pain. It couldn't swim, it couldn't fly – the arrow had broken one of its wings.

Siddhartha held his hands out to the injured bird, calling softly to calm it down. He held the bird tenderly in his arms and waded out to the riverbank. He quieted the swan, and then gently pulled the arrow out of its wing. Using a stick for a splint, and a strip torn from his clothing for a bandage, Siddhartha set and bound the wing of the swan.

Meanwhile, Devadatta came running up in search of his arrow. He too had seen the swans from a distance, and had decided to practice his shooting skills on the beautiful birds.

"That swan belongs to me," said Devadatta. "I shot it, not you."

"No," said Siddhartha. "It belongs to me. I saved it."

"Very well," said Devadatta. "Let us go to our guru. He will tell you that the swan is mine because it is my arrow that hit it!"

The two children took the injured swan to their guru. The guru heard Devadatta's tale and turned to Siddhartha.

"Well, Siddhartha," asked the teacher. "What do you have to say?"

"Devadatta hurt the swan," said Siddhartha. "The swan was doing him no harm! It was swimming in the river, looking so beautiful. Why did Devadatta shoot it? I will not let him have it, he will hurt it again. I have saved it from dying – so now it belongs to me."

The teacher smiled when he heard what Siddhartha had to say.

"The swan belongs to Siddhartha," he said. "Siddhartha has saved its life, and cared for it and gave a new life to the bird. Therefore, the swan should remain with Siddhartha".

Siddhartha has a peaceful smile on his face.

Moral: **Kindness is over the cruelty, always be kind to others.**

Source: **http://www.longlongtimeago.com/once-upon-a-time/myths/myths-from-india/siddhartha-and-the-swan/**

Annexure 8D

Value: Kindness **Activity: Word Puzzle**

KINDNESS AND WORD SEARCH

Name: ____________________

KINDNESS WORD SEARCH

H T D C O N S I D E R A T I O N

C D G N O T Y S S E N D O O G Y

L E U N D E R S T A N D I N G C

R E C Y C L E E E S O O H C N S

Y D I I S N L N Y T I N A M U H

I P O E T I S L O L R R C E U I

Y H H E M N D U U C L U Y D P N

C T E S T T V F I S U E O D I E

I W I D R E K P N I F C H C C V

S C D L U N E L E D I I E N A I

S Y M P A T H E T I C V A I L T

E O D H I I I H N H R R R T T I

N V T L W O D T A D E E T T R S

D O O G I N C R A L M S H G U O

N P E L Y T I S O R E N E G I P

I F R D C T E T D C G I L L S O

K D N A Y R A I N B O W P E M C

Find the following words:

recycle	choose	service	sweetness
rainbow	humanity	generosity	deed
helpfulness	good	consideration	help
choice	sympathetic	kindness	
smile	nice	charity	
gratitude	understanding	heart	
merciful	altruism	positive	
thankful	polite	love	
intention	courtesy	act	
goodness	cordiality	tolerance	

Source: https://www.google.co.in/search?q=KINDNESS+WORD+ SEARCH&rlz=1C2GNAM_en-

FORGIVENESS

SESSION 9
FORGIVENESS

9.1 DEFINITION

Forgiveness means to stop feeling anger and resentment about something, or towards someone who has done something wrong.

9.2 SESSION OBJECTIVE

- To develop an understanding of the concept and essence of the value of forgiveness.
- To discuss the importance of the value of forgiveness.
- To inculcate the value of forgiveness in children.

9.3 SESSION OUTLINE

Activity No.	Activity name	Duration
9.3.1	Preliminary Discussion	10 minutes
9.3.2	Art Attack	40 minutes
9.3.3	What Should I Do?	20 minutes
	Total Time	**1 hour 10 minutes**

9.3.1 Preliminary Discussion

(a) **Material Required:** Discussion Points.

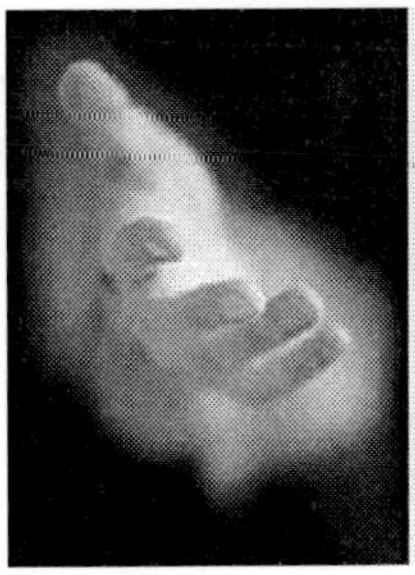

(b) Instructions: Tell the class that the topic of the day / the week is 'FORGIVENESS'. Write the term 'Forgiveness' on the board and facilitate a brief discussion around the following discussion points and their broad responses as should be expected:

(i) What do we mean by 'forgiveness'?

Forgiveness means to stop feeling anger and resentment about something, or towards someone who has done something wrong. It means to pardon someone and not seek revenge for what they did wrong.

By forgiving someone, you are not saying what the other person did is okay; but rather, that you have decided not to hold it against him/her. It may seem unfair to just let someone off without making them 'pay' for what they did. That is why it takes special kind of love and courage to forgive someone. In fact, forgiving someone shows strength of character, not weakness.

(ii) Why should we learn to forgive?

We should learn to forgive to make the world a better place. Everyone makes mistakes; so do we. But, if we learn to forgive people for their mistakes, they will feel more positive about changing their behaviour. In turn, they will like us better and their wlll be more peace, understanding, and kindness.

If we do not forgive, our feelings for others will become unfriendly because there will be so much anger and hurt in our hearts. We will also become crabby and miserable ourselves.

(iii) What if someone keeps hurting me?

Forgiveness does not mean that you should let the other person keep on hurting you. If someone keeps on being unkind or nasty, you should let someone in authority know about it. It could be your parents, a educator, or some other adult. Hurting others is not okay.

9.3.2. Art Attack

(a) Material Required:

(i) Drawing sheets

(ii) Crayons

(b) Instructions: Ask the students what makes them angry. Brainstorm some ideas in class and put them down on the board. Then provide drawing sheets and crayons to all the children. Ask them to draw a picture of someone or something that makes them very angry. Tell them that they could show their anger on their drawing, by turning the person who makes them angry into a dragon, or a monster, or an animal; or by scribbling all over them or by attacking them.

After all the students have done this, ask them to draw the same picture but in the light of forgiveness. Tell the students to forgive the person and draw his/her face with a smile, or showing happiness.

Now ask the students to compare their two drawings and note which one looks better. Reiterate on the message of how forgiveness makes the world a better and a happier place.

9.3.3. What should I Do?

(a) Material Required: Flash cards (provided in Annexure 7A).

(b) Instructions: Use the 5 sets of flash cards provided in Annexure 9A. Use the first card of the first set, and explain the situation to children – "your friend breaks your toy". Then ask the children how they will feel if this happens, and move on to what should they do if this happens. Show them the second card of this set, and display the scene that it would be like if they got angry. Ask them if they like the scene, and point out how negative both the people in the picture are looking. Now show them the third card of this set, and display the scene where forgiveness is involved. Ask them if they like the scene better, and point out the positivity and happiness in the scene. Reiterate on the message of forgiveness.

Repeat for all the remaining sets of scenes/situations provided in the annexure.

9.4 FOLLOW UP

1. Share simple stories of forgiveness with children. (Annexures 9B and 9C). Make sure to reiterate on the moral of the story, i.e. forgiveness, and discuss how it makes things more pleasant and happy.

Annexure 9A

Value: Foregiveness Activity: Discussion using Flash Cards

DISCUSSION USING FLASH CARDS

1. WHEN YOUR FRIEND BREAKS YOUR TOY

2. WHEN YOUR FRIEND ACCIDENTLY SPRAYS YOU WITH THE WATER HOSE

3. WHEN YOUR FRIEND LOSES YOUR MONEY

4. WHEN YOUR FRIEND LOSES YOUR DOG

5. WHEN YOUR FRIEND DROPS YOUR BIRTHDAY CAKE

Source: https://apps.ankiweb.net/

Annexure 9B

Value: Forgiveness **Activity: Story**

MARTY AND BRAD

Marty loved his brother, but his brother made him mad. He seemed to keep on doing things that made Marty feel bad. He took his radio outside and never brought it back. He ate the cookie Marty wanted to have for a snack.

He changed the TV channel in the middle of a show. He kept on being angry at his little brother Brad.

And every time his brother Brad came hoping to have fun, Marty complained about the bad things his brother had done. Marty refused to play with him, because he held a grudge. Brad said that he was sorry, but still Marty wouldn't budge.

Brad tried and tried to make amends, to get Marty to play; but Marty said, "I'm mad at you, and you should go away!" So finally Brad gave up. He went outside to play alone, and Marty watched him from the window playing on his own.

Brad kicked a ball around the yard while looking very sad. Then Marty thought, "What did Brad do that really was so bad?" He did say he was sorry, but Marty would not forgive,and now his angry grudge affected how the brothers live.

They both were quite unhappy, and they both were all alone. Marty learned just how wrong he was to have a heart of stone. He started feeling sorry for the things that he had done. He hoped Brad would forgive him, so they both could have some fun.

He forgot all the bad things Brad had ever done before. And being with his brother seemed to matter so much more. So Marty went outside and found Brad underneath a tree.He said, "I'm sorry Brad. Do you think you can forgive me?"

Then Brad said, "Forgive you? I thought that you were mad at me!" They both forgave each other. It was such a sight to see.They kicked the ball together, and had fun out in the yard. They learned that to forgive each other is not very hard.

It does no good to hold a grudge, or push other away. It's best to put the past behind and make a better day. But then Brad kicked the ball and it hit Marty in the head. Brad thought he would be mad again, his face was turning red.

But Brad said he was sorry, and Marty said, "That's okay. I guess we're lucky. I learned how to forgive you today."

Moral: Forgiveness is important to maintain happy relationships.

Source: http://ikhaa.edu.lb/cms/assets/files/summer%20stories/ stories%20grade%201.pdf

Annexure 9C

Value: Foregiveness **Activity: Story**

THE BRIDGE

Once there were two brothers who were great friends and always played together. However, one day they had a huge argument about one of their toys. In the end, they decided that from then on they would only be allowed to play with their own individual toys.

They had so many toys and things that they agreed to spend the next day sorting out which toy belonged to whom. So, the next day each brother got to work, making a pile of his own things. When they had finished doing the big toys it was time to sort the little stuff. However, they had already taken so long that it was time for bed, so, they left the small toys for the next day. The same thing happened the next day, because they had started dividing up parts of the house.

Day after day it was the same story. They were spending their whole time deciding what, among all kinds of things, belonged to either one of them. Anything would set them off: seeing an animal, a tree, or even a stone. In the end, they had accumulated two complete mountains of stuff which had to be kept out in front of the house.

As the years passed, nothing changed: every morning they would meet up to argue about which things belonged to whom. They were getting older, and everyone now knew them as "the grumpy old men". No one had ever seen them smile.

That was, until one morning they went out and found that their two mountains of stuff had been totally mixed up together. Someone had been there, mixing their things up! After all that time and effort they had spent to separate everything!

Furious, the brothers tried to find who had done it. Soon they found few children playing on the other side of the mountains of stuff. They were happily playing together, picking everything up, careless of whether they were mixing it all together. They looked really happy, enjoying themselves fully.

Seeing the children so happy, the two grumpy old brothers realized how foolish they had been for so many years. They had given up playing with anything, instead spending their whole lives arguing over what was theirs to play with. How sad they felt, for spending their lives in anger. At the same time, though, they were happy to have finally realized their foolishness.

They spent that day, and the rest of their days, playing together with those two children, mixing everything up, and sharing it all. People even stopped calling them the grumpy old men. Now, people called them the 'Big Kids'.

Moral: Learn to forgive and appreciate what you have.

Source: http://www.ba-bamail.com/content.aspx?emailid=25711

OBEDIENCE

SESSION 10
OBEDIENCE

10.1 DEFINITION

Obedience is the quality of being obedient, which describes the act of carrying out commands. Obedience differs from compliance, which is behaviour influenced by peers; and from conformity, which is behaviour intended to match that of the majority.

10.2 SESSION OBJECTIVE

- To develop an understanding of the concept and essence of the value of obedience.
- To discuss the importance of the value of obedience.
- To inculcate the value of obedience in children.

10.3 SESSION OUTLINE

Activity No.	Activity Name	Duration
10.3.1	Preliminary Discussion	10 minutes
10.3.2	Chintu Says	15 minutes
10.3.3	Mother May I?	30 minutes
10.3.4	Everyone Help Me	45 minutes
	Total Time	**1 hour 40 minutes**

10.3.1 Preliminary Discussion

(a) Material Required:

(i) Discussion Points.

(b) Instructions: Tell the class that the topic of the day/the week is 'OBEDIENCE'. Write the term 'Obedience' on the board and facilitate a brief discussion around the following discussion points and their broad responses as should be expected:

(i) What do we mean by 'obedience'?

Simply put, obedience means "doing what you are told to do – all the way, right away, and with a happy heart". Obedience is based on the principle of trust – meaning that you completely believe and trust the person in authority for demanding/asking the right thing of you.

(ii) Why should we learn to obey?

Obedience is important, most prominently, for our own protection and safety. When a person in command gives us directions to do something, it is most probable that they know better than we know. For example, if my mother asks me to do something around the house, I should obey her because she is in charge of the house and understands the needs of the house better than I do. Similarly, if my educator asks me to keep quiet in class, I should obey because she is in charge of class and I may not be understanding as well how I may be disturbing the class. In these situations, I should obey so that I am abiding by the law and so that I don't get in trouble (my mother will not complain to my father or will not spank me for being bad; my educator will not punish me or report to the principal).

Obedience also helps to make us stronger. Obeying someone doesn't show weakness; it shows strength because we let the other person take charge, and perform well in their commands as well.

10.3.2 Chintu Says

(a) Material Required: None.

(b) Instructions: One of the people is "it" – i.e. Chintu. The others must do what Simon tells them to do when asked with a phrase beginning with "Chintu says". If Chintu says "Chintu says jump", the players must jump (players that do not jump are out). However, if Chintu says simply "jump", *without* first saying "Chintu says", players do not jump; those that do jump are out. In general, it is the spirit of the command, not the actions that matters; if Chintu says "Chintu says touch your toes", players only have to show that they are *trying* to touch their toes. It is the ability to distinguish between valid and invalid commands, rather than physical ability, that matters here. It is Chintu's task to try to get everyone out as quickly as possible, and it is everyone else's job to stay "in" for as long as possible.

Now begin with becoming Chintu yourself (to make the game more clear to children), and ask the children to follow the appropriate commands. After a few rounds, involve one of the children to become Chintu. Try to make as many children as possible Chintu, after a couple of rounds each, in the given period of time.

10.3.3 Mother may I?

(a) Material Required: None.

(b) Instructions: One player, particularly a female (but sometimes a male) plays the "mother" or "father". The other players are the "children". To begin the game, the mother or father stands at one end of a room, while all the children line up at the other end. The children take turns asking "Mother/Father, may I ____?" and makes a movement suggestion. For example, one might ask, "Mother/Father, may I take five steps forward?" The mother/father either replies "Yes, you may" or "No, you may not do that, but you may ____ instead" and inserts his/her own suggestion. The players usually move closer to the mother/father but are sometimes led farther away. Even if the mother/father makes an unfavourable suggestion, the child must still perform it. The first of the children to reach the location of the mother/father wins the game. That child then becomes the mother/father himself, the original mother/father becomes a child, and a new round begins.

10.3.4 Everyone Help Me

(a) Material Required:

(i) Cleaning supplies.

(ii) Decorating supplies.

(b) Instructions: Tell the class that you need to clean and decorate the classroom today, and you need the help of all students to do so. Also tell them that you have only 20 minutes to do this. Then, one by one, give directions to them about cleaning and decorating the classroom. These directions could be —

(i) Set your desks and chairs in order and in line. No desk or chair should be non-aligned.

(ii) Set all your bags on your chairs neatly.

(iii) Clean the educator's desk and put the chalks and dusters in place.

(iv) Ensure that no books, stationery or anything else is on any desk in the classroom.

(v) Put up charts to cover all the bulletin boards in class.

(vi) Sweep any dust or dirt in the class.

Now ask the children if the classroom looks better to them. Also, thank them for helping you out.

Follow this up with a discussion about how well the children obeyed or didn't obey you. Ask them how it would have been if one child didn't obey you or a group of children didn't obey you. Talk about how this would have disrupted the order and prevented you from reaching your goal. Reiterate on the value of obedience and appreciate children for their strength and character.

Note: This particular exercise can be taken up for a variety of tasks such as the following, or any other.

(a) Cooking something.

(b) Cleaning the garden.

(c) Making a construction/model.

10.4 FOLLOW UP

1. Tell the students the story of the dutiful son Ram (from *Ramayana*), explaining how he fulfilled his father's command by going to exile for 14 years. Share how this made him such a revered king and an emblem of character, even though he had to go through a lot of trouble. Refer to Annexure 8A and Annexure 8B for cues.

Annexure 10A

Value: Obedience	**Activity: Story**

THE DUTIFUL SON—RAMA

Long long ago, in India, there lived a king whose name was Dasharatha. He ruled the kingdom of Ayodhya (part of present day Uttar Pradesh) from its capital Ayodhya. He was loved by one and all because he cared for the happiness and prosperity of his subjects. Dasharatha had three queens, Kaushalya, Kaikeyi and Sumitra. Even though Dasharatha had everything to make him happy he was very sad at heart because had no children.

He was getting old, and was worried for not having an heir to inherit his throne.

Upon the advice of his *guru* (spiritual guide), Vashishtha, Dasharatha performed a great sacrificial fire worship. On the final day of worship, a figure appeared in the huge flame with a bowl of rice pudding. The figure intoned, "Take this rice pudding and divide this amongst your wives. They will give you the sons you desire." Then it disappeared.

Dasharatha took the bowl to his first wife, Kaushalya, and gave her half of the pudding. Out of what was left, he divided that to his second wife Kaikeyi and the third wife Sumitra. When a little bit of pudding was still in the bowl, he gave that to Sumitra saying "Here, finish it up."

Kaushalya duly gave birth to a son, Rama. Kaikeyi was next, with a son Bharat. Sumitra was the last. She had been given two helpings, so she had twin boys, Lakshmana and Shatrughna.

As the boys grew older, Lakshmana got attached to his eldest brother, Rama, and Shatrughna to Bharat. All the brothers, however, were very close and loved each other. Rama was respected by all because of his good nature and truthful character. He was strong, handsome and was the heir to the throne.

When the boys were close to sixteen, it was one day, sage Vishwamitra arrived in the court of Dasharatha.

Vishwamitra requested Dasharatha to send Rama and Lakshmana with him to the forest to kill the demons who disturbed him in his prayers. Rama and Lakshmana accompanied the sage and killed the she-demon Tadaka and her followers. Vishwamitra was pleased and taught Rama the sacred verses to call for the divine weapons to be used to protect justice.

After completing the task, Rama was ready to return home when Vishwamitra asked Rama to accompany him to the kingdom of Janak. Janak's eldest daughter, Sita, was about to pick a husband from the princes assembled in the *swayambara* (a gathering arranged for choosing a royal husband).

Almost every prince present in the assembly wanted to marry Sita as she was the most beautiful girl on earth. To choose the best of the princes in the gathering, a condition was laid. Sita will marry the prince who will be able to bend and string a very heavy bow left in front of the assembly.

One after another all princes tried to lift the bow, but it could not be lifted, let alone bend and string. It weighed like a mountain.

Finally, Janak was about to give up when Vishwamitra asked Rama to try. Rama took his blessing, prayed, and lifted the bow at ease. When he tried to string the bow it snapped in two.

Rama proved to be the strongest prince in the assembly. Sita happily garlanded him. Dasharatha was informed and he requested Janak to let the three sisters of Sita marry his other three sons—Lakshmana, Bharat and Shatrughna. Janak was overwhelmed with the unexpected offer from Dasharatha. He immediately made all arrangements and all the four brothers got married together in front of the sacrificial fire.

Dasharatha then decided to retire making Rama the crown king of Ayodhya. But things did not go according to Dasharatha's plan.

When the day of coronation of Rama was announced, Bharat and Shatrughna were at their maternal uncle's place. The city started to prepare for the occasion and the queens were happy for the oncoming event. At this time, Dasharatha's second wife Kaikeyi got an ill advice from her scheming, hunchback maid Manthara.

Manthara said to Kaikeyi, "Why are you happy in celebrating Rama's coronation? Don't you realize that you will not be as respected as Kaushalya and Bharat will be totally ignored." "What nonsense you talk," said Kaikeyi, "I love Rama and he is the heir." "Not if you change things" said Manthara in a devilish voice. "But, how can I?"

"Easily," said the scheming maid, "Remember, a very long ago, you saved Dasharatha's life during a war, and he said he would grant you any two wishes." "Yes, and I said I would ask for my wishes later, when I knew what I wanted," said Kaikeyi. "Exactly" shouted Manthara, "Ask for them now. Ask for Bharat to be crowned king and for Rama to be banished to the forest for fourteen years."

Kaikeyi fell a prey to the conspiracy of Manthara. When Dasharatha came to accompany her to the coronation ceremony, she was lying on the floor, sobbing.

When Dasharatha repeatedly asked the queen about the thing that was bothering her, Kakeyi replied, "Do you recall the promise you made, when I saved your life in the battle field, to fulfill two of my wishes?"

"Yes my queen" said Dasharatha, "I remember that and I will not break my promise. Ask for what you desire!"

Kaikeyi sternly said, "Crown Bharat king and banish Rama to the forest for fourteen years."

King Dasharatha was stunned into silence. He or his ancestors had never broken a promise. What could he do now? His happiness and his future had all been stolen from him instantly.

Dasharatha some how whispered to his attendant, "Go and get Rama." When Rama arrived, his father was far too unhappy to speak. It was Kaikeyi who spoke, "Bharat is to be king and you are to be banished for fourteen years."

"Is this what my dear father desires?" asked Rama.

"Your father is keeping his two promises to me," Kaikeyi answered.

"Then I have no choice, I must honour my father's word. If promises are made, they must be kept. Let Bharat rule. I leave for the exile immediately."

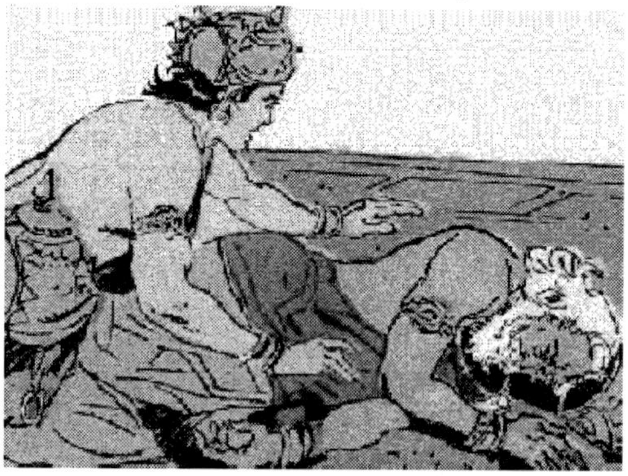

Sita and Lakshmana insisted to accompany Rama.

Dasharatha died shortly following Rama's departure.

When Bharat came to know about this he got furious with his mother and Shatrughna kicked Manthara out of the house. Then Bharat went after Rama in order to request him to come back and rule the kingdom. Rama very humbly refused as he did not want his father's promises to be broken. Bharat returned to Ayodhya with Rama's sandals and ruled the kingdom as an appointee of Rama. Even in the palace he chose to lead the life of a hermit like his elder brother Rama.

During the exile, Sita was abducted by the demon king Ravana.

Rama hunt out Ravana with the help of the monkey king Sugreeva and his commander Hanuman. A fierce battle ensued and Ravana was finally defeated. Rama triumphantly returned to Ayodhya with Sita after fourteen years' of exile. We celebrate Diwali in memory of Rama's return to Ayodhya.

Rama is considered by all Indians as an ideal son who willingly undertook hardship in order to save his father's honour. He was also a great warrior and an emblem of justice.

Moral: True wisdom of God is born out of obedience. We should always obey our elders.

Source: http://www.indolink.com/Kidz/rama.html

PATIENCE

SESSION 11
PATIENCE

11.1 DEFINITION

Patience refers to the willingness to wait, without complaint.

11.2 SESSION OBJECTIVE

- To develop an understanding of the concept and essence of the value of patience.
- To discuss the importance of the value of patience.
- To inculcate the value of patience in children.

11.3 SESSION OUTLINE

Activity No.	Activity Name	Duration
11.3.1	Preliminary Discussion	10 minutes
11.3.2	Patient Thinking	30 minutes
11.3.3	Stick Pick	40 minutes
	Total Time	**1 hour 20 minutes**

11.3.1 Preliminary Discussion

(a) Material Required:

(i) Discussion Points.

(b) Instructions: Tell the class that the topic of the day/ the week is 'PATIENCE'. Write the term 'Patience' on the board and facilitate a brief discussion around the following discussion points and their broad responses as should be expected:

(i) What do we mean by 'patience'?

Patience refers to the quality of not giving up, showing loss of temper, or irritation, when faced with difficult circumstances, provocation, annoyance, misfortune, or pain. It is also the ability or willingness to suppress restlessness or annoyance when confronted with delay. When everything is going our way, patience is easy to demonstrate. The true test of patience comes when our we face difficulties and obstacles in life.

(ii) Why should we learn to be patient?

Patience is a virtue for various reasons:

- It helps us to understand the value of something. For example, I may really like to eat chocolate, but I need to be patient to get chocolate sometimes in life. If somebody gave me chocolate all the time, and I had chocolate to eat all day long, then I will get bored of it and not like it any more. I will not understand how nice chocolate is and what a treat it is to have one.
- Patience also helps us to better accept our circumstances. When I am patient, I can be more accepting of what is going around. For example, if I don't have a new school bag, I need to be patient to get one in the future. If I show that patience, then I will feel better and look forward to getting it when I can. However, if I am impatient, then I will feel bad everyday when going to school, because I will not be able to wait to have a new school bag.
- Patience affects our relationships with those around us. If I will be impatient, then I will get angry/upset, and other people may not perceive me nicely. This will, in turn, affect my relationships with them. For example, if I want to sit on a swing, but some other child is sitting on the swing, then I must show patience until it is my turn to get on the swing. If I do that, the child who is on the swing and my other friends will like me. But, if I just show impatience, I will probably show anger towards the swinging child, or get frustrated with

him/her, or hit her. Then everyone will think of me badly and my friendships will get badly affected.

(iii) What are the situations in which we should show patience?

As written above, patience should be shown in a variety of situations. In fact, it should be in our nature, so that it can be present in each and every aspect of our lives. Some of the broad situations in which we should practice patience are:

- Classroom (wait for our turn to answer etc.)
- Home (wait to get things etc.)
- Playground (wait for our turns etc.)
- Public settings (wait in line to go to the bathroom etc.)
- Relationships (not get angry with people too soon etc.)

11.3.2 Patient Thinking

(a) Material Required: None.

(b) Instructions: As a class, have students identify things that are hard to wait for. Discuss it for about 5-10 minutes, giving many children chances to speak, so that they can all relate to something or the other.

After this, ask the students to close their eyes and take deep breaths as they imagine waiting for something (such as opening a gift, eating dinner, or having a turn on the swing). Tell them all to pick one such situation they feel for, and imagine what it feels like to wait for it. Maybe, they are thinking about tearing open the gift wrap, or gobbling up all the yummy food, or making the child on the swing fall so they can get their turn sooner. Then instruct them to imagine showing patience, and how that feels. Like, maybe, they can turn their attention away from the gift, so that they can open it when they are alone later, or in peace; or they can wait to eat food and imagine savouring each bite of the yummy food their mother gave them; or roam around in the rest of the playground until it is their turn to get on the swing. Ask them to deep breathe while imagining patient waiting. After 30 seconds of deep breathing, tell the students that the time they are waiting for is getting closer and that they have 10 more seconds to wait. Remind the students to continue to breathe deeply as you count backwards from 10, and they come closer to what they have been waiting for. Once you reach one, instruct the students to open their eyes.

Have a talk about the breathing exercise and how it helped them deal with the waiting.

11.3.3 Stick Pick

(a) Material Required: Bunches of many toothpicks or pencils.

(b) Instructions: Keep bunches of toothpicks/pencils ready. (There should be 3-4 times the number of toothpicks/pencils as the number of children playing the game.) Tell the children that we are going to play a game that requires a lot of patience and skill. To demonstrate, hold the bunch of toothpicks/pencils together with your hand on a wide desk/space, in an upright position. Then carefully remove your hand so that all the toothpicks/pencils fall in a disarray in the given space. The rule of the game is to pick up toothpicks/pencils, one-by-one, and by turn, in a way that it does not move any other toothpick or pencils in the lot. If somebody manages to pick up a toothpick/pencil, then they get a chance to pick another one, and it keeps going on until they end up moving something else in the process. In that case, the next person in turn gets a chance. However, if somebody moves the other toothpicks/pencils when trying at first, the game directly moves on to the next person. The game continues until all the toothpicks/pencils in the centre have been picked up. The person who ends up with the most number of toothpicks/pencils wins the game.

Note: If you have a smaller class of students, you may play this game with all of them together. However, if your class has more than 20 children, it will be better to divide them in groups, and give them a bundle of toothpicks/pencils each, so that they can play in an appropriate group-size.

11.4 FOLLOW UP

1. Share simple stories of patience with children. (You may use the stories provided in Annexure 11A, Annexure 11B and Annexure 11C) Make sure to reiterate on the moral of the story, i.e. patience, and discuss how it bears fruit.
2. Use Annexure 11D to provide children worksheets, in which they can find the pattern and discover a beautiful picture if they work patiently.

Annexure 11A

Value: Patience **Activity: Story**

PAYS

Once, a king had announced that anyone who wanted the post of personal assistant must meet him. Many people gathered in the palace. The king led them to a pond and said, "Whoever will fill this pond's water in this pot will be chosen for the post. But remember, there is a hole in the pot."

So, some people left without a single try. While some people tried and said, "The king has already chosen someone else. Let's go."

But one man kept filling the pot with pond water patiently. He filled the water in the pot from the pond and came out on the ground. But within a few moments, the water poured on the ground completely. He put it uncountable numbers of times. At last the pond was empty. The man found a diamond ring in the empty pond and he gave it to the king. At this the king said, "This ring is a reward for your patience and hard work. You are fit for the job."

Moral: **Patience is not the ability to wait, but how you act while you are waiting.**

Source: **http://www.english-for-students.com/Patience-Pays.html**

Annexure 11B

Value: Patience **Activity: Story**

JUDGEMENT AND PATIENCE

A Father and his Daughter were playing in the park. His daughter spotted an apple vendor. She asked her father to buy her an apple. Father didn't bring much money with him, but it was enough to purchase two apples. So, he bought two apples and gave them to his daughter.

His daughter held one apple each in her two hands. Then the father asked her if she can share one apple with him. Upon hearing this, his daughter quickly took a bite from one apple. And before her father could speak, she also took a bite from the second apple.

The Father was surprised. He wondered what mistake he made raising her daughter that she acted in such a greedy way. His mind was lost in thoughts, that perhaps he is just thinking too much, his daughter is too young to understand about sharing and giving. A smile had disappeared from his face.

And suddenly his daughter with an apple in her one hand said, "Father have this one, this one is much juicier and sweeter". Her father was speechless. He felt bad about reaching to the judgement so quickly about a small child. But, his smile came back now knowing why his daughter quickly took a bite from each apple.

Moral: Don't judge anything too quickly and reach a conclusion. Always spare time to understand things better.

Source: https://www.moralstories.org/lesson-hastening-judgement/

Annexure 11C

Value: Patience **Activity: Story**

ANT AND KARAN

Once upon a time there was a small boy named Karan who didn't like to study. He always found one excuse or the other when asked by his mother to sit and study. He lost concentration from one activity to the other very fast. His parents spared no efforts to help him but at the endthey were always left disappointed. Karan received regular scolding from his mother, father and other siblings. His arguments with the family were always based on the plea that he was too small to learn remember and understand lessons in the books.

Once he was sitting near the garden after being scolded for not studying, when he saw a small ant carrying food in her small mouth. The size of food was a little larger than the mouth of the ant. She took few steps and the food dropped from her mouth. The ant picked it up again and crawled further few more steps. The boy looked at the sight engrossed, as the ant continued to crawl slowly again and again till she reached her destination with the food intact in her mouth.The boy who was watching it closely clapped loudly. His mother who was sitting next to him looked at him surprised.The boy seemed delighted. He questioned his mom "Mumma if I study small portions at a time and revise the last learnt lesson again and again and be patient, Will I be able to remember my assignments?". The mother was over joyed with his question and replied "Yes patience and persistence can make us win in all situations". The lesson which she could not teach him by preaching had been learned by the little Karan, while watching the ant who did not give up easily.

Moral: Patience Pays!

Source: Author's creations.

Annexure 11D

Value: Patience **Activity: Pattern**

PATIENCE PATTERN SEARCH

Name: ____________________

Can you see what this picture is? Colour each number a different colour to find out!

1 — Orange	5 — Red
2 — Yellow	6 — Green
3 — Purple	7 — Brown
4 — Blue	8 — Black

Source: https://www.education.com/worksheets/identify-continue-shape-patterns/

RESPONSIBILITY

SESSION 12
RESPONSIBILITY

12.1 DEFINITION

Responsibility refers to the value of being accountable for what you do; for your actions and your behaviour.

12.2 SESSION OBJECTIVE

- To develop an understanding of the concept and essence of the value of responsibility.
- To discuss the importance of the value of responsibility.
- To inculcate the value of responsibility in children.

12.3 SESSION OUTLINE

Activity No.	Activity Name	Duration
12.3.1	Preliminary Discussion	10 minutes
12.3.2	What If...?	30 minutes
12.3.3	Responsibili-tree	40 minutes
	Total Time	**1 hour 20 minutes**

12.3.1 Preliminary Discussion

(a) Material Required: Discussion Points.

(b) Instructions: Tell the class that the topic of the day/the week is 'RESPONSIBILITY'. Write the term 'Responsibility' on the board and facilitate a brief discussion around the following discussion points and their broad responses as should be expected:

(i) What do we mean by 'responsibility'?

Responsibility means accountability – you must be accountable for your behaviour and answer for your actions. Responsibility further means trustworthiness – you must be dependable when you have things to do, and take care of your duties.

(ii) Why should we be responsible?

Being responsible is very important. It is a core value for living honourably. Being responsible is important because:

- It helps us take care of ourselves and of other people around us. For example, if I have the responsibility to take care of my dog, then I must do that...give it food, take it for a walk etc. If I am not responsible and slip up on taking care of my dog, then I will end up hurting it in one way or the other. Similarly, if my responsibility is to complete my homework, then I must do it to avoid getting in trouble at school.
- It also helps to keep order in our society. This is so because everyone gets assigned different responsibilities, which in turn helps everyone. For example, at home, my father may be responsible for earning money, and my mother may be responsible for taking care of the house — this helps both my father and mother and me, and keeps the order of our house. Similarly, at school, my educator is responsible for teaching me and I am responsible to study. If my educator doesn't fulfil her responsibility, then I will not learn anything, and if I don't study, then I will fail.

(iii) What are the different types of responsibilities?

There are many different kinds of responsibilities that we have in life. These are:

- Personal Responsibility (for things that I have been assigned to do everyday – like homework, helping my mother etc.).
- Family Responsibility (for things that I must do for my family – like take care of my parents when they get old. Spend time with my grandparents, etc.).

- Legal Responsibility (for my state, country etc. – like pay taxes when I get old etc.).
- Community Responsibility (for the good of my community – like help to keep it clean, vote when I get old etc.).
- Global Responsibility (for the entire Earth – like to stop harming the environment, not cut trees etc.).

(iv) How can we be responsible?

Some examples of how you can be responsible are –

- Complete your homework and chores on time without being reminded.
- If you commit to do something, make sure you complete it even when you don't feel like it.
- Accept responsibility for your mistakes and learn from them. Don't make excuses or blame others.
- Take care of your things and those of other people. Return items you borrow.
- Find out what needs to be done and do it.
- Make wise choices, such as choosing to eat healthy foods and wearing a helmet.
- Always do your very best.

12.3.2 What If...?

(a) Material Required: List of "what if..." questions.

(b) Instructions: Divide the class into different groups/teams. Tell them that you will be asking them a series of "what if" questions, and each team will get points depending on how well they answer. Ask the following questions, one-by-one, and score the teams on how well and descriptively they answer. (Use probing, if necessary, through the first 2-3 questions. Encourage children to think about multiple consequences of each statement.)

- What if the farmer who grew the wheat (of which our *roti*/bread is made) decided to play cards instead of harvesting the grain?
- What if the farmer who raised animals for meat decided he was just too tired to take the animals to the market?

- What if the person who owns the shop where we buy daily things from didn't feel like working for a few weeks and played with friends instead?
- What if our milkman decided it was too cold to deliver milk for a few weeks?
- What if our mother decided she was too busy to take care of us?
- What if our math educator decided that it was just too boring to teach children how to count and add, and didn't come to school for a few months?
- What if the cleaners/janitors in the school decided that they didn't like their work and stopped working for a whole month?
- What if the police personnel responsible for our community decided that they didn't like our community and stopped taking care of keeping criminals out of our community?

Ask the children if they understand what can happen when people do not show responsibility. Explain that we count on others to be responsible and do their job correctly and on time, and likewise they also have jobs that are just as important. (Ask the students to give examples of their jobs.) Conclude the activity by sharing that when you do what is expected of you to the best of your ability, then you are being responsible and others can count on you!

12.3.3 Responsibility—Tree

(a) Material Required:

(i) Drawing sheets

(ii) Crayons

(iii) Leaf-shaped stencils of green paper

(iv) Glue

(b) Instructions: Give students a drawing sheet, and ask them to draw a tree trunk on the base of it. Allow some time so that children can draw and colour their trunk. Follow this up with providing about 5-8 leaf-shaped stencils to each child, and ask them to glue these leaves above their tree trunk, to form a beautiful tree. Instruct the students to write their most significant responsibilities – one on each leaf of the tree. (Provide examples like filling up bottles of water at home, taking out the garbage, finishing lunch etc.) Tell them that this is their "responsibili-tree" – that they should remember their responsibilities and follow through on them.

Note: If possible, you may want to display the responsibility-trees made by children in the classroom. This will work as a positive reminder.

12.4 FOLLOW UP

1. Share simple stories around responsibility with children. (You may use the stories provided in Annexure 12A.) Make sure to reiterate on the moral of the story.
2. Use Annexure 12B to provide children worksheets, in which they can complete the columns about responsibilities of different people around them.

Annexure 12A

Value: Responsibility Activity: Story

CARELESS CLOWN

There was once a clown named Lemon. He was able to do a lot of fun, but was always very careless. Whenever he did anything, he almost always ended up tearing his jacket, getting a hole in his sock, or ripping the knee of his trousers. Everyone said he should take more care, but Lemon did not listen. One day,he had the happy idea of buying himself a sewing machine. This machine was so fantastic that it sewed everything up within a moment. It seemed like Lemon wouldn't have to worry about his torn things anymore.

Soon, the most important day in Lemon's life arrived. It was the day when everyone in town prepared a party for him, in celebration of Lemon's many years of service in making the people chuckle. On that day he wouldn't have to wear his colourful clown suit. That day he would be dressed like anyone else.

However, the night before, he had a look in his closet, and there wasn't a single suit in good condition. They were all ripped and torn, with dozens of stitching marks. Lemon couldn't possibly go to the party dressed in those. So, he attended the gala celebration in his usual clown suit. This amused the audience, whereas Lemon could not really be happy though he was being awarded on that day. On the very next day, Lemon replaced all those damaged old suits with the new ones from the money given to him as reward and since then, he decided to look after his clothes with great care. He realized that using short-term remedies ends up being no remedy at all.

Moral: Responsibility is the most important ability that the person can possess.

Source: https://freestoriesforkids.com/children/stories-and-tales/careless- clown

Annexure 12B

RESPONSIBILITIES WORKSHEET

Name: ________________

The following chart lists different occupations. Write the responsibilities of each person (in Column 1), and what could occur if that person was irresponsible (in Column 2).

Job	Responsibilities	What could happen if they were irresponsible
Teacher		
Fire fighter		
Plumber		
Father		
Student		
Gardener		

SINCERITY

SESSION 13

SINCERITY

13.1 DEFINITION

Sincerity implies eagerly doing what is right, with transparent motives.

13.2 SESSION OBJECTIVE

- To develop an understanding of the concept and essence of the value of sincerity.
- To discuss the importance of the value of sincerity.
- To inculcate the value of sincerity in children.

13.3 SESSION OUTLINE

Activity No.	Activity name	Duration
13.3.1	Preliminary Discussion	10 minutes
13.3.2	What A Deal!	40 minutes
13.3.3	Sincere Card Making	40 minutes
	Total Time	**1 hour 20 minutes**

13.3.1 Preliminary Discussion

(a) Material Required: Discussion Points.

(b) Instructions: Tell the class that the topic of the day / the week is 'SINCERITY'. Write the term 'Sincerity' on the board and facilitate a brief discussion around the following discussion points and their broad responses as should be expected:

Annexure 13A

Value: Sincerity **Activity: Story**

PRINCESS DIANA

Diana, Princess of Wales had a compassionate heart for children and that was evident in the charity work in which she was involved.

After attending finishing school in Switzerland, she moved to London where she had several jobs, all involving children. Diana also received recognition for her support of the International Campaign to Ban Landmines. Her interest in landmines was focused on the injuries they create, often to children, long after a conflict is over. During her final year Diana lent highly visible support to the International Campaign to Ban Landmines, a campaign which won the Nobel Peace Prize in 1997, only a few months after her death.

From 1989, she was the president of the Great Ormond Street Hospital for children, in addition to dozens of other charities. Also in 1989, while she was visiting Harlem Hospital in New York City, she was photographed hugging a 7-year old AIDS patient. She wanted to show that it was safe to touch an AIDS patient, something that was still feared at that time.

The Princess of Wales was a devoted, imaginative and demonstrative mother. She was involved in much of the daily activities of her sons as often as her schedule permitted. She also negotiated her public duties around their timetables.

When her royal duties required her to travel to other countries, she always took time to schedule visits to charitable organizations that ministered to children or infants. She was most interested in interacting with the children directly rather than executive tours. She often returned want to say 'I love you' to their parent or grandparent, they may want to thank somebody who did something for them, they may want to give a compliment to their friend etc. Then provide drawing sheets and other material to children, asking them to make a sincere greeting card, saying what they want, to the person of their choice. Keep reminding them about doing it from their heart, and not out of any gain or fear or competition or compulsion. Tell them to sincerely make the greeting card, thinking about the receiver.

Appreciate them for their sincerity and ask them to give their greeting cards to the intended persons.

Note: Allow the children to make more than one card if they sincerely wish to do so.

13.4 FOLLOW UP

1. Share with children the story of Princess Diana (the Princess of Wales in England), for being a model of sincerity. Use Annexure 13A for reference.

the educator will pat us on the back, then we are not being sincere. But if we study because we actually want to do well, and learn, and be educated, then we are being sincere.

13.3.2 What a Deal?,

(a) Material Required: A deck of playing cards.

(b) Instructions: Draw the following table on the board.

CLUB	HEART	SPADE	DIAMOND

I sincerely want to ...	**I sincerely love...**	**I sincerely think I'm bad at...**	**I sincerely think I'm good at...**

Instruct the children that you will give them a playing card each, and they will have one of these signs made on them. Depending on what is made, they must complete the statement that matches, after thinking about it for a few seconds. They must use the word "sincere" and make sure it is coming from their heart – sharing it with the rest of their class.

Go around the class and conduct the activity. Encourage children to be sincere and also respectful to each other.

13.3.3 Sincere Card Making

(a) Material Required:

(i) Drawing Sheets

(ii) Crayons

(iii) Sketch Pens

(iv) Pens/Pencils

(v) Any other material for making greeting cards

(b) Instructions: After recalling the previous activity and discussion on sincerity, ask the students to think about who they sincerely want to say something to. Give them ideas in the form of examples – they may

(i) What do we mean by 'sincerity'?

Sincerity is all about our hearts – that our insides are right. Many character traits can be worked on from an external perspective – like we can act responsible by coming to school everyday, or we can show kindness by petting a dog. In this way, we can do the right thing through our actions. But sincerity looks at our heart – our motive of doing something. It means that we should not do something for the show of it, but purely from the heart.

(ii) When should we be sincere?

Sincerity should be in our nature, and we should show it in all our roles –

- we should be sincere students and study because we want to learn and we want to be educated.
- we should be sincere children of our parents and love them from our heart.
- we should be sincere people and be grateful and thankful to all those around us who help us.
- we should be sincere friends and be nice to our friends from our heart.

Like this, we should be sincere in all that we do – when we compliment someone, when we are trying to learn a new skill, when we greet someone etc.

(iii) How can we be sincere?

We can be sincere by having the right motives. To do this, we must always think why we are doing something good –

- Are we doing it out of fear for the consequences?
- Are we doing it because we think we'll get something from it?
- Or are we doing this because it is the right thing to do?

For example, when we study out of the fear that our parents will scold us if we don't study, we are not being sincere. If we study because

BIBLIOGRAPHY

Brainy Quotes. http://www.brainyquote.com/quotes/quotes/j/jiddukrish395484.html (Retrieved on 5 August, 2012)

Brannon, D. (2008). Character education—A joint responsibility. *Education Digest*, 73: 56-60. Retrieved November 7, 2008, from Professional Development Collection Database.

Carson, C. (ed.) (1998), *The Autobiography of Martin Luther King*, Intellectual Properties Management Inc. and Warner Books, New York, USA.

Central Board of Secondary Education, *Value Education: A Handbook for Teachers*. New Delhi, CBSE (1997 and 2003).

Gandhi, M. (1940), *My Experiments with Truth*, Navajivan Publishing House, Ahmedabad, India.

Kohlberg, https://www.simplypsychology.org/kohlberg.html; by Saul McLeod, published 2011, updated 2013. (Retrieved on 3rd March, 2017).

Lincoln, A. (1905), *The Autobiography of Abraham Lincoln*, F.D. Tandy Company, New York.

National Council of Educational Research and Training, *Values Education in Indian Schools: Experiences and Strategies of Implementation*. New Delhi, NCERT (2003).

Spink K., *Mother Teresa: A Complete Authorized Biography* (1998), Harper Collins Publishers, New York, USA.

Thornberg, R. (2006). Hushing as a moral dilemma in the classroom. *Journal of Moral Education*, 35: 89-104.

United Nations Educational Scientific and Cultural Organization, *Learning the Way of Peace—A Teacher's Guide to Peace Education*. New Delhi, UNESCO (2001).

to these charities after the cameras left to more fully interact with children.

Diana's sincere devotion to her own children and the children of the world came from her heart and her actions reflected that.

Moral: Sincerity is the basis of every virtue.

Source: https://in.pinterest.com/pin/238761217714741227/?lp=true